SIGNS

The Significance of Biblical Prophecy

SIGNS

The Significance of Biblical Prophecy

NEIL MACKERETH

Signs: The Significance of Biblical Prophecy

Published by Neil Mackereth.

Published using KWS services. www.kingdomwritingsolutions.org

ISBN 978-1515016762

CONTENTS

APPENDICES

PREFACE

The seeds of this book were sown when I was asked to run an End Times Study Course at Winchester Vineyard Christian Fellowship. In my research for the course I became increasingly aware of how little I really knew and understood about fulfilled prophecy and about the signs and indications that I am now convinced God is providing for our direction and encouragement in the world today.

This new awareness led to a further realisation that if I did not know what the Bible says about the future—the prophecies yet to be fulfilled—I would have no idea whether world events were unfolding in random fashion or were following a course that has been foretold. In other words, I became aware that my ignorance could be my downfall.

The journey has absorbed and enthused me to the extent that now my hope is that others will be captivated by the thread of amazing signs and predictions relating to past, present and future events that show God's involvement in, and His overarching plan for, mankind.

For this book I have drawn on notes I prepared for the End Times Course, and those written in the past for teaching, preaching and essays, as well as summaries made at seminars and at meetings. I have also gleaned information from books read long ago, from Christian TV programmes, teaching tapes, CDs, DVDs etc, etc, etc (to quote from *The King and I!*).

I am therefore indebted to a great number of people, some of whom I am able to name, without being able to specify the exact source, and others whose input I regret I am unable to acknowledge. Those who have influenced my thinking, with respect to End Times theology, include Derek Prince, Mike Bickle, Chuck Missler, David Pawson, Wayne Grudem, and David Hathaway.

I am not an academic and this is the first book I have ever written. Having no experience in researching or referencing material, but being aware that there must be copyright requirements, I looked to other writer's books in the hope of some inspiration. I have been reading the magnificent and meticulously sourced *Jerusalem* by Simon Sebag Montefiore (Phoenix 2012) and come to realise that the work of referencing and the building of a bibliography are way beyond my capability, even for a book as small as this.

I then turned to the introduction to *Unlocking the Bible Omnibus* by David Pawson (Collins 2003). There David writes, "I can only offer an apology and my gratitude to all those whose studies I have plundered over the years, whether in small or large amounts, hoping they might see this as an example of that imitation that is the sincerest form of flattery."

Having scratched my head and explained my dilemma, I beg the indulgence of any holder of a copyright that I may have infringed and I apologise in advance.

I must add my heartfelt thanks to my friend Peter Davey, who has tirelessly read the drafts and suggested corrections and improvements, his input and support have been invaluable. I am also greatly indebted to Mark Stibbe for the professional editing and wise counselling that he has provided.

I close this preface with a comment on the signs of the times. As I write, in July 2014, the situation is very tense in Israel and the Arab world. Furthermore the western world is facing unprecedented political, economic and spiritual upheaval. These global currents lead me to say that I am convinced that we should do our utmost to try to understand the times in which we live. Astonishing as it may seem, much of what is happening today appears to have been predicted in the Bible!

The pace of world events is such that any commentary is likely to be overtaken by new developments within hours of being written. Some may feel that the speed of change undermines the topicality, and hence the relevance, of a book of this nature. For me the opposite is true; it simply increases the urgency and necessity to identify and explain the underlying significance of global events and trends.

That is why I have written this book. My aim is to examine a number of signs of our times as well as biblical prophecies. Having looked at these past predictions and contemporary real-time world events, I will let you—the reader—conclude whether or not prophecy is being fulfilled in our day.

Neil Mackereth

Winchester

Introduction: GETTING OUT OF THE WAY

In Genesis 24:27 (KJV) we read the simple statement: "I, being in the way, the Lord led me."

In the original context these words were spoken by a faithful servant called Eliezer who is on a quest to find an appropriate bride for his master's son. Eliezer is given his mission. He then asks questions and determines his options, prays for guidance, makes his plan (which allows for variation as events progress), makes appropriate administrative and logistical arrangements, sets off expectantly, watches for signs, accepts confirmation thankfully, explains the situation to the interested parties, avoids unnecessary delay, and carries the mission through to completion.

Eliezer's example here is commendable. He works with military precision. His methods are sound. His heart is loyal. His objectives are fulfilled.

He is truly a faithful servant.

This Scripture has been very relevant in the writing of this book about the signs of the End Times. In the King James Version Eliezer says, 'I, being in the way.' 'In the way' can mean 'en route' (i.e. on the required journey). It can also carry the connotation in the English language of obstructing someone from achieving their goal.

Have you ever been 'in the way' of what God has been trying to do in your life?

The fact is that for some time I was *in the way*. In other words, my own thoughts, opinions and preconceptions were getting in the way of the Lord's direction for my writing. It was as if my ideas about how this book should look and what it should say were forming a logjam, preventing a free flow of the river of revelation in my heart. The "I" was in the way.

Writing this book has been a lesson in becoming a faithful servant.

In terms of its content, I have had to let go of a lot of my ideas about the End Times and the Second Coming. 'I, being in the way,' had to get out of the way!

Perhaps a brief reference to Sherlock Holmes is helpful here. Holmes once castigated his sidekick Dr Watson with these words: 'You see but you do not observe.' This is how I was before I prepared and led the End Times course and then started writing this book. I had been seeing what was going on in the world but I had not been *observing*. In other words, I had not been interpreting what I was seeing in the light of Scripture.

This tendency to see with the natural eyes rather than observe with eyes enlightened by revelation is what needed to be removed. This is part of the 'I' that was in the way of God's work in my life.

Jesus repeatedly encouraged his disciples to observe not just see, especially in regard to the signs that would point to the climax of history. In Matthew 24 and Mark 13 his emphasis on watching, being on one's guard, staying alert and recognising signs of the end of the age, is a theme that runs through both chapters. Jesus also emphasised being in the light (knowing what Scripture means in its original setting and what it signifies today) that we might be aware of contemporary events that are the fulfilment of ancient prophecy.

For decades I have described myself as a Christian, but I had no idea about most of the information I bring to your attention in this book. I have accepted, far too readily, what I was told by eloquent and persuasive speakers, often agreeing with the most recent theories without recognising that it contradicted what I had enthusiastically accepted from a previous speaker! I went further and ignored subjects that I was told were far too difficult or only for doom-mongers.

In recent times, however, my mind has been renewed. I have got out of the way. My preconceptions and my prior pet theories have been removed. All this has paved the way for the Lord to lead me, through His Word and by His Spirit, into a fresh understanding of both ancient prophecy and current events in the world.

'I, being in the way, the Lord led me.'

I am not saying that everything I write here is God's Word. Only the Bible can claim that level of inspirational authority and accuracy. What I would say is that there are observations in this book that I ask you to consider. Come to your own conclusions. Try not to be 'in the way' of God leading you. Let His Holy Spirit guide you as you read, giving you clarity about the meaning and significance of the many biblical prophecies I reference in the coming pages, and eyes to see how they may be finding their fulfilment in what is going on in the world today.

Resolve to move the 'I' out of the way and allow the Lord to lead you.

It is the pathway to becoming a faithful servant.

Part 1: Setting the Scene

Chapter 1: MIRACULOUS PREDICTIONS

If you had a book, written long ago, which included detailed descriptions of momentous future events, and then they happened, wouldn't you want to shout that fact from the rooftops?

If it could be shown that the foretelling had been absolutely accurate, wouldn't you want to confirm the book's authenticity and study its predictions about events yet to be fulfilled?

When I suggest that there is such a book, people often seem genuinely interested; but when I say "it's the Bible," there tends to be an "oh" of disappointment. Why is that?

What do we need to do to draw people's attention to these astonishing and supernatural truths?

Maybe we are not "marketing" this extraordinary reality effectively.

I believe that world events and the Bible's forecasts show such an astonishing correlation that the alignment cannot be ignored. I am also convinced that God gives us indicators that are designed to make us think about the spiritual implications of the things that are happening around us. We will look at some of these signs in later chapters.

For ease of navigating our journey, I have divided the book into five parts:

1. An introduction to the topic, with some guidelines and

ground rules to help attain a reasonable level of objectivity, and including a consideration of the pitfalls and challenges to fair and impartial study.

2. An overview of aspects of the histories of Israel and Babylonia, as a foundation for considering their significance in Biblical prophecy and its fulfilment.
3. An assessment of where we are on the timeline of Biblical prophecy, with reference to some examples of fulfilled prophecy in the period of Jewish history called "The Exile" (6th century BC). I will also consider the prophecies fulfilled by the advent of Jesus (1st century AD).
4. A focus on aspects of End Times prophecy.
5. A look at the significance of current events in relation to Biblical prophecy and a consideration of what is yet to happen.

It has to be admitted that there is often an overlap between past and current events and this means that the content of our discussion may not be as neatly compartmentalised as this five-part structure implies. At the same time this will not prevent us from trying to discern the connections across the fields of investigation and assessing their spiritual significance.

In all of this I want to capture your imagination and open your eyes to the awe-inspiring revelation of Biblical prophecy.

Ten Scriptures Prophesying Israel's Rebirth

Right at the outset I want to whet your appetite by looking at some amazing examples of fulfilled prophecy from recent history. I will do this using ten Scriptures that prophesy the re-establishment of Israel as a nation. This momentous event happened in 1948—thousands of years after the prophecies were given and recorded. I will provide brief comments and approximate dates in my discussion of these parallels.

1. *"I will bring back my exiled people Israel; they will rebuild the ruined cities and live in them. They will plant vineyards and drink their wine; they will make gardens and eat their fruit. I will plant Israel in their own land, never again to be uprooted from the land I have given them," says the Lord your God.*

   Amos 9:14-15 (written 760 BC)

The prophet Amos, writing some 2750 years ago, foresaw the return of his dispersed and exiled people to their homeland. The short-range fulfilment occurred in 536 BC, after the Jewish people deported to Babylon ("The Exile", which will be considered in more detail in subsequent chapters) were allowed back to the land of their forefathers. This was the more immediate fulfilment. But Biblical prophecy often contains a dual focus—an immediate or shorter term fulfilment in history and an ultimate or longer term fulfilment at the culmination of history.

The long-range fulfilment of this prophecy happened in 1948 when the Nation of Israel was miraculously re-established, leading to an ingathering of Jewish people from their two thousand year Diaspora (dispersion throughout the world). Note that the prophecy makes clear that they will not be displaced again.

2. *"So I prophesied as he commanded me, and breath entered them; they came to life and stood up on their feet—a vast army. Then he said to me: "Son of man, these bones are the whole house of Israel. They say, 'Our bones are dried up and our hope is gone; we are cut off.' Therefore prophesy and say to them: 'This is what the Sovereign Lord says: O my people, I am going to open your graves and bring you up from them; I will bring you back to the land of Israel. Then you, my people, will know that I am the Lord, when I open your graves and bring you up from them. I will put my Spirit in you and you will live, and I will settle you in your own land. Then you will know that I the Lord have spoken, and I have done it, declares the Lord.'"*

   Ezekiel 37:10-14 (written 580 BC)

Once again there is an immediate and an ultimate fulfilment contained within the same prophecy. Ezekiel, prophesying in the 6th century BC, foresees the revival of the Jewish people as a nation. At the time they were languishing in Babylon, what we now call Iraq. But within fifty years the Jewish people—numbering about 50,000—were allowed back to their own land and to the site of the ruined Temple in the sacked city of Jerusalem. By the turn of the century the new Temple had been built and the nation had been resurrected through the work of the Holy Spirit (Zechariah 4:6).

However, in AD 70 Jerusalem and its Temple were destroyed once again, this time not by the Babylonians but by the Romans. Once again the Jewish people were exiled from their homeland and scattered across the globe as displaced people living as minority groupings in numerous countries.

How the Jewish people didn't die out completely is a miracle!

Ezekiel saw this and predicted an even greater miracle—the resurrection of the Jewish people in the End Times. This occurred when Israel re-established sovereignty in 1948, three years after the end of the Holocaust, during which it is estimated that one in three Jews was killed by the Nazis.

It seems to me that Israel was brought back from the dead!

3. *"Before she goes into labour, she gives birth; before the pains come upon her, she delivers a son. Who has ever heard of such a thing? Who has ever seen such things? Can a country be born in a day or a nation be brought forth in a moment? Yet no sooner is Zion in labour than she gives birth to her children."*

   Isaiah 66:7-8 (written 700 BC)

This prophecy is quite remarkable in its accuracy, although this should not be startling given that God inspired the prophet who decreed it! The description of a woman giving birth before going into labour is a very apt analogy for what happened on 14 May 1948 when modern Israel was "born in a day", only to face the onslaught of its enemies.

On that day, the United States recognised Israel's sovereignty. The United Nations mandate expired, ending British control of the land. Over a 24-hour period, foreign control of that part of Palestine ceased and Israel declared its independence as a nation.

Israel was born in a single day!

As Ezekiel prophesied, the labour pains followed. Egypt, Jordan, Syria, Lebanon, Iraq and Saudi Arabia attacked Israel within hours. Israel's declaration of nationhood had triggered a war. On 15th May 1948, Azzam Pasha, the Secretary General of the Arab League, said: "This will be a war of extermination and a momentous massacre which will be spoken of like the Mongolian massacres and the Crusades." Others made similar comments during the war of 1948-49, and during the 1967 and 1973 wars, and the rhetoric continues.

Nevertheless, Israel survives!

4. *"And say to them, 'This is what the Sovereign Lord says: I will take the Israelites out of the nations where they have gone. I will gather them from all around and bring them back into their own land. I will make them one nation in the land, on the mountains of Israel. There will be one king over all of them and they will never again be two nations or be divided into two kingdoms."*

Ezekiel 37:21-22 (written 580 BC)

When this was written Israel had been divided into two kingdoms—Israel in the North and Judah in the South. The original undivided kingdom was formed from the federation of twelve Israelite tribes that occupied Canaan (an area roughly corresponding to the Levant, a historical geographical region which covered what we now know as Lebanon, Israel, the Palestinian territories, west Jordan and south west Syria) in the time of Joshua. This kingdom was first established under King Saul (c 1050 to 1010BC), consolidated and strengthened by King David (1010 to 970BC) but divided into northern and southern kingdoms after the death of King Solomon (970 to 931BC). Why did this division occur? The ten northern tribes rebelled against Solomon's son and successor Rehoboam (931 to 914BC) while the tribes of Judah and Benjamin remained loyal. The ten rebellious tribes became Israel (the northern kingdom), the two loyal tribes became Judah (the southern kingdom).

Once again we see both a shorter term and a longer term fulfilment of this prophecy. While the shorter-term fulfilment occurred towards the end of the 6th century BC, when the scattered Jewish people returned from their bleak exile in Babylon, the longer-term fulfilment occurred in 1948 when Israel was reborn as a single nation and the dispersed Jewish people began to return to what is known as *Ha Aretz*, the Land. Although the people only occupied a fraction of the area of the former "Land of Canaan", we can still see remarkable resonances between Ezekiel's words in the 6th century BC and events in the Middle East in the twentieth century.

5. *"However, the days are coming," declares the Lord, "when men will no longer say, 'As surely as the Lord lives, who brought the Israelites up out of Egypt,' but they will say, 'As surely as the Lord lives, who brought the Israelites up out of the land of the north and out of all the countries where he had banished them.' For I will restore them to the land I gave their forefathers.*

   Jeremiah 16:14-15 (written 600 BC)

This promise of the restoration of the Jewish people to their homeland was not only fulfilled in the time of the return to Judah in the 6th century BC. It was also fulfilled in the twentieth century, and its fulfilment continues! After 1948, Jews have returned to Israel, after nearly 2000 years of dispersion, from as far afield as Russia, China, the United States, the United Kingdom, Africa and many other continents and nations.

It seems Jeremiah was operating with both an immediate and an ultimate prophetic vision.

6. *I will bring them out from the nations and gather them from*

the countries, and I will bring them into their own land. I will pasture them on the mountains of Israel, in the ravines and in all the settlements in the land.

Ezekiel 34:13 (written 580 BC)

Once again this occurred both in the 6th century BC and in the 20th century AD. Since 1948, millions of "exiles" have returned to Ha Aretz.

7. *"Hear the word of the Lord, O nations; proclaim it in distant coastlands: 'He who scattered Israel will gather them and will watch over his flock like a shepherd.'*

   Jeremiah 31:10 (written 600 BC)

It is in our own times as it was in Jeremiah's (6th century BC): God is watching over the re-established Nation of Israel. Israel has survived and succeeded against enormous odds.

8. *"You will pursue your enemies, and they will fall by the sword before you. Five of you will chase a hundred, and a hundred of you will chase ten thousand, and your enemies will fall by the sword before you."*

   Leviticus 26:3, 7-8 (written 1400 BC)

The day after Israel's declaration of independence in 1948, Egypt, Syria, Jordan, Iraq, and Lebanon invaded. The combined population of those countries was more than 20 million at that time whilst Israel had fewer than 1 million. Even so, Israel won and increased its size by 50 %.

Similar examples of memorable victories against enormous odds can be seen in the 1967 "6 Day War" and the 1973 "Yom Kippur" war.

9. *Then the Lord your God will restore your fortunes and have compassion on you and gather you again from all the nations where he scattered you. Even if you have been banished to the most distant land under the heavens, from there the Lord*

your God will gather you and bring you back. He will bring you to the land that belonged to your fathers, and you will take possession of it. He will make you more prosperous and numerous than your fathers.

Deuteronomy 30:3-5 (written 1400 BC)

Israel is amazingly prosperous, in relation to its size, as evidenced by this quote from a Jewish newspaper of 5th July 2011:

"Very few countries have managed to grow and prosper so quickly in 60 years, from a standard of living of $3,100 per person in 1948 to today's $25,000; from a country of 600,000 residents to 7.3 million; and from an orange exporter to an international high-tech power".

10. *I dispersed them among the nations, and they were scattered through the countries; I judged them according to their conduct and their actions. And wherever they went among the nations they profaned my holy name, for it was said of them, 'These are the Lord's people, and yet they had to leave his land.' I had concern for my holy name, which the house of Israel profaned among the nations where they had gone. "Therefore say to the house of Israel, 'This is what the Sovereign LORD says: It is not for your sake, O house of Israel, that I am going to do these things, but for the sake of my holy name, which you have profaned among the nations where you have gone. I will show the holiness of my great name, which has been profaned among the nations, the name you have profaned among them. Then the nations will know that I am the LORD, declares the Sovereign LORD, when I show myself holy through you before their eyes. 'For I will take you out of the nations; I will gather you from all the countries and bring you back into your own land'.*

Ezekiel 36:19-24 (written 580 BC)

This scripture is very significant, particularly for those who wonder why God would re-establish and watch over the mainly secular state of Israel. The reason is because He said he would. It is for His name's sake (for the honour of His name). The Abrahamic Covenant is an everlasting covenant, which God will fulfil, not for the sake of His unruly people Israel but to show the world He is God, His name is holy, and He always honours all He has promised and, of course, there is more to come!

The Miracle that is Israel

So there you have it! Ten Scriptures from the Old Testament, written between 3500 and 2500 years ago, all of which predict the unforeseen and improbable return of the Jewish people to the Land and the prosperity that would greet them when they did. All this is nothing short of miraculous!

Perhaps the most miraculous thing of all is the very survival of the Jewish people since their Temple and city were destroyed in AD 70. Think about it! For the next two thousand years—until 1948—the Jewish people survived in pockets and as "lodgers", sometimes integrating, sometimes not, in all corners of the world. Their tribal identity outlived great dynasties and mighty empires! As Mark Twain famously commented:

"If the statistics are right, the Jews constitute but one percent of the human race. It suggests a nebulous dim puff of star dust lost in the blaze of the Milky Way. Properly the Jew ought hardly to be heard of, but he is heard of, has always been heard of. He is as prominent on the planet as any other people, and his commercial importance is extravagantly out of proportion to the smallness of his bulk. His contributions to the world's list of great names in literature, science, art, music, finance, medicine, and abstruse learning are also away out of proportion to the weakness of his numbers. He has made a marvellous fight in the world, in all the ages; and has done it with his hands tied behind him. He could be vain of himself, and be excused for it. The Egyptian, the Babylonian, and the Persian rose, filled the planet with sound and splendour, then faded to dream-stuff and passed away; the Greek and the Roman followed, and made a vast noise, and they are gone; other peoples have sprung up and held their torch high for a time, but it burned out, and they sit in twilight now, or have vanished. The Jew saw them all, beat them all, and is now what he always was, exhibiting no decadence, no infirmities of age, no weakening of his parts, no slowing of his energies, no dulling of his alert and aggressive mind. All things are mortal but the Jew; all other forces pass, but he remains. What is the secret of his immortality?"

(Mark Twain "Concerning The Jews," Harper's Magazine, 1899)

Isn't it incredible that so many Biblical prophecies, foretelling Israel's re-gathering, were so accurately realised by the re-establishment of the nation of Israel in 1948? And isn't it even more astonishing that most people, including Christians, have no idea that contemporary events are staggeringly accurate fulfilments of prophecies made and recorded some 2,500 to 3,500 years ago? Surely there can only be one explanation for why so many are blind to this truth. Someone is trying to keep us from seeing the significance of what is written in Scripture, and from understanding how it relates to world events.

It's time to remove the veil.

It's time to see!

Chapter 2: TAKING THINGS LITERALLY

The label on the bottle said, "Before giving the baby milk, boil it."

Now there's an example of how it would be extremely dangerous to interpret a statement too literally!

Perhaps in this instance, as in so many others, we need to add a dash of common sense to any assessment of whether something is intended to be taken literally or metaphorically.

Sometimes it is obvious when a statement is metaphorical. Sometimes the author tells us whether the statement or passage is to be taken literally. At other times the intent of the author is unclear.

In this chapter and the next, I want to look briefly at how we interpret biblical prophecy, and specifically how we know when prophecy is meant to be understood literally or figuratively.

The Telescope Effect

The Bible is full of metaphors. Detailed study and informed research may be necessary before we can assess a Biblical author's meaning. And even then, the meaning of a passage may be so open to personal interpretation that it becomes the basis of much learned debate, sometimes convoluted and acrimonious in nature.

Chapter 1 was a trailer for all this and in it I used prophecies about the rebirth of Israel as a nation as an indicator of the accuracy, reliability and reality of Biblical prophecy.

My belief is that the events of 1948 have particular significance. For nineteen hundred years many theologians have developed and refined principles for the allegorical interpretation of Scripture, taking a figurative rather than a literal view of Biblical texts. However, the re-establishment of Israel has turned the metaphorical approach on its head. What was before assumed to be metaphorical turned out in the fullness of time to be literal. Israel's delivery and birth was not a metaphor for national restoration; it was a literal prophecy referring to actual events in space and time.

Be warned, however. To almost any view you or I might hold, or assumption you or I might make, there is likely to be a counter opinion. So, for example, there are some who would disagree with my view in chapter 1, Stephen Sizer among them (see his book *Christian Zionism*). In their opinion, Old Testament prophecies about the re-gathering of the dispersed Jewish people and their return to Israel do not refer to some literal re-establishment of the nation of Israel in our own day. They claim that while these prophecies might have found a literal fulfilment after the Exile (in the 6th century BC), they have no relevance to the events of 1948.

My view, and the view of many others, is that Biblical prophecy often has both an immediate and an ultimate historical reference. In other words, Biblical prophecy has a fuller sense than people like Stephen Sizer allow. At one level, Biblical prophecies find partial fulfilment in a shorter-term or immediate event or series of events. At another level, Biblical prophecies find their complete fulfilment in a longer-term or ultimate event or series of events, in the End Times of history.

Perhaps the most obvious example is in Matthew 24, a chapter in which Jesus prophesies catastrophic events in the future. Some of these prophecies were fulfilled about 40 years later when Jerusalem was sacked by the Romans and when the Jewish Temple was destroyed (AD 70). Other prophecies were not fulfilled in AD 70. They will be fulfilled at the climax of history, the time-frame I'm calling 'the End Times.'

This telescopic effect of short and long distance fulfilment is one of the most compelling and mysterious characteristics of Biblical prophecy.

In my view, Old Testament prophecies of the return of the Jewish people to the Land have both an 'already' and a 'not yet' quality to them (as has the Kingdom of God). Those who only see the immediate application are too short-sighted. Those who only see the ultimate application are too long-sighted. I believe in a "both-and" approach.

In this book I am simply going to look at Biblical prophecies and contemporary events and let you, the reader, determine whether or not we are seeing a literal fulfilment of these predictions in our own times.

Levels of Prophecy

The word 'prophecy' in the Bible refers to someone who speaks on behalf of God, under the inspiration of the Holy Spirit. In our own time, those who follow Christ are filled with the same Spirit that inspired the prophets of the Bible. The Holy Spirit, if you will, is the spirit of prophecy. That is why the Apostle Peter, on the Day of Pentecost, said that the outpouring of the Holy Spirit upon the church is the Spirit that empowered believers to have dreams and visions—in short, to prophesy! One of the Biblical evidences of being filled with the Holy Spirit is therefore that a believer is empowered by God to speak on His behalf, declaring to others what their eyes have seen and their ears have heard as their Father in heaven has revealed His heart and shared His thoughts with them. As far as the Apostle Paul is concerned, every follower of Jesus can prophesy but not everyone does prophesy.

Does this mean that every follower of Jesus has the same ability and authority when it comes to prophecy? The New Testament answers this with a clear "no." According to the Apostle Paul, there are degrees of prophetic authority. At level 1 there are those who simply have a *gift* of prophecy. All believers are urged to desire the gift of prophecy. All believers can therefore operate in a rudimentary way under a prophetic anointing, seeing visions and dreaming dreams, receiving messages and words from the Father about the church, about others, about themselves.

At level 2 there are those who graduate beyond the gift of prophecy to the *ministry* of prophecy. Such people are recognised by the church as having a track record of accurate prophecies coupled with Christ-like character. They are given permission and freedom to speak out the revelations they receive, respecting the guidelines laid out in 1 Corinthians 14.

Then at level 3 there is the *office* of the prophet. This is someone set apart by the church, usually as a result of faithful and fruitful ministry as a prophet, to a leadership role within the local church. This person represents the prophetic gift on the leadership team. He or she can also often be called to be an itinerant prophet to churches within the same stream as their own, and even to the nations.

So there are degrees of prophetic authority:

LEVEL 1: THE GIFT OF PROPHECY

LEVEL 2: THE MINISTRY OF PROPHECY

LEVEL 3: THE OFFICE OF PROPHECY

What this highlights is the simple fact that every one of us has a Biblical responsibility to grow in the gift of prophecy. While not all of us are going to have a ministry or an office of prophecy, all of us are called to covet the gift and to hear what the Father is saying.

This means, among other things, knowing the signs of the times!

Not Missing the Signs

Jesus underlined the significance of Biblical prophecy when He held the Pharisees accountable for not recognising its fulfilment when their own eyes were witnessing it: "You did not recognise the time of God's coming to you," Jesus says to them in Luke 19:44.

Jesus was angry with the religious leaders of His own day because they knew the prophecies about the coming of the Messiah but when He, the Messiah, was in front of their very eyes they failed to see that prophecy was being fulfilled literally in their midst.

The Bible clearly teaches that the Messiah Jesus was not only going to enter history once (His First Coming, born as a baby in a manger) but twice (His Second Coming, returning on the clouds with great glory, with the hosts of heaven in his fiery wake).

If so many Biblical prophecies were fulfilled in His First Coming, we can expect the applicable prophecies to be fulfilled in His Second Coming too.

And literally!

Furthermore, if Jesus was angry with religious people for missing the signs of prophetic fulfilment surrounding His First Coming, how much more will He be angry with those who miss the signs of prophetic fulfilment surrounding His Second Coming!

Let me give you some interesting and sobering statistics.

There are about 270 prophecies in the Old Testament foretelling the first Coming of Jesus, all of them fulfilled literally.

There are 1845 Old Testament prophecies and 318 New Testament prophecies that foretell His Second Coming.

Isn't it both logical and reasonable to suppose that these will also be literally fulfilled?

So we should be vigilant. As the Apostle Peter says: "We have the word of the prophets made more certain, and you would do well to pay attention to it, as to a light shining in a dark place, until the day dawns and the morning star rises in your hearts" (2 Peter 1:19).

What does "more certain" mean? Usually things are either certain or not certain. In this case I believe Peter is saying that, since he had seen with his own eyes many prophecies fulfilled in the First Coming of Jesus, then we can surely be *more* certain that the remaining prophecies will be fulfilled in His Second Coming.

My aim in this book is not to write a learned thesis on every single one of these prophecies concerning the Second Coming. Rather it is to draw your attention to significant events and trends in the world today and to set these alongside Biblical prophecies. I will do this using plain English rather than convoluted academic language. I will also leave you to do further research and come to your own conclusions whether current events and trends are what the title of my book suggests—SIGNS!

Before we get into the meat of the book, however, there is one niggling issue that I'm sure you'll be thinking about already.

How can I be sure that what I'm discerning is correct?

How can I guard against a purely fanciful and subjective interpretation of the signs of the times?

How can I build my views on objective truth rather than personal preconceptions?

It is to these important questions that we turn in the next chapter.

Chapter 3: OUR CONFIRMATION BIAS

I remember playing as a child on the beach at Seaton Carew. On the foreshore there was a huge factory of interweaving, hissing and steaming pipes and chimneys. An enormous sign said: "SULPHURIC ACID WORKS."

My thought was "why would you make it if it didn't?"

Much later, as an officer cadet in Aldershot, I was scrubbing the steps of the Guardroom when the Regimental Sergeant Major stopped and said, "I want you to get up to the Commandant's residence and water his lawn."

"But Regimental Sergeant Major, Sir, it's raining," I replied

"Well wear your raincoat!" he retorted.

My point in these anecdotes is that the interpretation of information, seen or heard, differs with each recipient's perception. Between the sending of a message and the receiving of it there is a filtering process in which the receiver tries to *interpret* the message sent. Receiving the message in an accurate, responsible and faithful way depends on the receiver perceiving the intentions of the sender. In both instances above, a receiver failed to understand the intentions of a sender. Sometimes it is only later on that a person realises that they misunderstood or only half understood the signals that someone was sending.

Looking in the Right Direction

In the coming chapters we are going to look at some facts and events that I find thought-provoking and which seem to have escaped the notice of many people. Before we get there, however, I want to consider some of the challenges we face in trying to ensure that material is presented in a fair and balanced way.

The significance of information we receive when we see or hear words varies from person to person. It is this diversity of human responses that makes room for people to misinterpret messages sent by others, leading them down cul-de-sacs of wrong conclusions. These false conclusions can often be frivolous; occasionally they can be dangerous.

A couple of years ago my wife and I went on a wonderful cruise up the Amazon. There was a Fitness Centre on one of the lowest decks of the ship and most days I would go down to take some exercise.

The treadmill machine faced a wall with a huge screen that showed the view from a camera on the bridge. I would walk on the treadmill, for half an hour at about 4 mph, watching our progress up the Amazon.

One day I realised that the screen was on a rear bulkhead and hence I was facing the stern. So the appearance of walking forward up the Amazon was an illusion: I was actually facing backwards (and going nowhere at 4 mph) while the ship carried me upriver at about 6 knots!

In this case my false conclusions about the information I was receiving were frivolous. But it is not hard to imagine that, in different circumstances, such misconceptions or delusions could easily lead to serious or dangerous consequences!

The RAS Factor

The basic problem was this: I had arrived at a perception of reality which I was not prepared to question. In other words, I had embraced what is known as 'confirmation bias.'

Confirmation bias is the tendency to seek out information that supports any hypothesis that one may have and, conversely, ignore information that runs counter to one's particular theory or proposition.

The more we want something to be true, the more likely we are to filter out opposing evidence. Warren Buffett, the famous American businessman and philanthropist, once said: "What the human being is best at doing is interpreting all new information so that their prior conclusions remain intact."

This tendency to be selective may operate at a subconscious as well as a conscious level. A while ago my wife and I were looking to buy a new car. We decided we liked the VW Tiguan. Amazingly we started seeing VW Tiguans everywhere we went, as if confirming that our choice was a good one! Surely all these Tiguans were a sign that we were meant to have this particular model of car!

This phenomenon is due to a process carried out in a part of the brain known as the Reticular Activating System (RAS). The RAS takes instructions from your conscious thoughts and acts like a filter into the subconscious.

For example, the "instruction" may be something like, "look for evidence to support buying a VW Tiguan." The RAS then acts like a gatekeeper to your conscious mind, allowing confirmatory information and disallowing negative data. Our conscious thoughts program our RAS and our decisions then get confirmed by a one-sided internal debate. In other words, our RAS looks for things that favour and confirm what we want to believe or do. We fool ourselves into only seeing what we want to see; we seek and find evidence to support our desires. I should add that this is very much a layman's understanding of what is undoubtedly a very complex psychological process!

Don't Spin the Data

There are few topics more vulnerable to confirmation bias than discussion of the signs of the End Times. It is very easy to come to a view on a certain aspect of the climax of human history, as prophesied in Scripture, and then to trawl the Internet for data that supports the view adopted, however subjective and outlandish that may be. Books about the End Times are especially prone to this danger. Authors with a particular confirmation bias simply ignore counter-evidence and counter-arguments and prefer instead to focus exclusively on material that supports their particular theory. At its worst this has led to authors and preachers predicting that the world will end on such-and-such a date, only to find that the world continues on apace without either Christians disappearing (a view known as the Rapture) or Christ appearing (the Second Coming).

Unfortunately most Christians are not helped in this regard by their own social contexts. Most of us live in cultures where political leaders are constantly using data to confirm a certain bias. This tendency, referred to as "spin" in the political arena, does not help us when it comes to responsible thinking on matters of far greater importance, such as the signs of the times and the end of history. If we are to embrace an honest and objective perspective on a topic of this global and ambitious scale, then we will need to be very conscious of our own confirmation bias.

This is especially important in contemporary culture where a view known as 'relativism' has been widely embraced. This is the view that says that nothing is absolutely true anymore. Everything is relatively true.

I hear people using expressions like: "that's your perception, not mine." "You have your truth; I have mine." "Everyone needs to find their own truth; that may be true for you but it is not true for me."

This is 'relativism.'

I meet people who believe that they are Christians, and also believe in astrology, or reincarnation, or they practice psychic healing, or see God as some sort of universal life force present in all matter.

Some Christians believe in divine judgement and some do not.

Some believe that Christians go to heaven when they die and some don't.

Some that there is, or will be, a hell, and some that there is not, and won't be.

These are but a few random examples.

The point is that I have had many conversations with people who have ideas that are, in my view, contradictory, illogical or mutually incompatible. For example, those who say that there are no longer any absolutes and that everything is relatively true are guilty of a grave self-contradiction. In the very act of saying there are no absolutes they make an absolute claim (the claim that there are no absolutes!). In denying something, they use the very tactic they are denying!

That is illogical!

At best it is lazy thinking. At worst it is downright deception!

Interpretation and Integrity

But it is not just non-Christians who believe and promote this nonsensical kind of thinking. Christians do it too. When those who claim to follow Christ start treating the Bible as a 'pick'n'mix' store, selecting those parts that they find sweet and rejecting those they find distasteful, then they need to realise that they too have become relativists. They are using the Bible as if some of it is true rather than all of it.

Followers of Christ seek to imitate Christ. We do not find the Christ of the Gospels indulging in a relativistic view of the Hebrew Bible (the Old Testament). He does not speak as if some parts are true and others less true. Rather He reveres the Scriptures and uses them as the baseline for His thinking and the foundation for His teaching. This is because He knows that all Scripture is God-breathed. In every passage, His Father in heaven inspired people so they could be the faithful mouthpieces and recorders of His words to His people and indeed to the world. When Christians imitate

Christ and honour the Bible as 'true truth', they will look to search the Scriptures in a rigorous and honest way when investigating any topic, including that of the End Times. They will seek to interpret the Bible with the help of the same Spirit who inspired it. This in turn will promote objectivity.

This chapter has been something of a health warning. If we want something to be true, we need to be very careful to ensure that we examine all the evidence, for and against, in a systematic and balanced way. Awareness of confirmation bias will help us to avoid the pitfall of being inappropriately selective. In other words, integrity is vital. We should seek to be like the "noble Bereans" in the Book of Acts (Acts 17:11), who listened eagerly to what was being said by Paul the Apostle and then diligently searched the Scriptures for confirmation.

In our case we can go further than the noble Bereans and use "search engines" and study guides to explore topics in considerable depth. We have what the Bereans did not have—rapid access to a wealth of detailed research. But the Bereans may have had what we lack—the virtue of nobility which involves honest and honourable research.

As I take you on this journey, don't therefore take my word for anything. If something intrigues you, conduct your own research, bearing in mind your own confirmation bias.

But above all be noble like the Bereans. Consider all the evidence and be open to the truth.

Chapter 4: WHAT IS TRUTH?

When Pontius Pilate looked into the eyes of Jesus, he asked a question that remains as relevant as ever: "What is truth?"

There are so many answers to that question. Among the most common would be: 'truth is what is true for you as an individual." "Truth is what everyone in a room agrees is true." 'There is no such thing as truth because truth is an absolute term and there are no absolutes anymore." Maybe you've heard these comments. Maybe you've made them yourself!

From these assertions it is plain to see that truth has taken quite a hit in recent decades. We are living in times when people no longer accept that any one group of people has a monopoly on the truth. In fact people have become cynical about the very idea of truth.

At the same time many, especially in Western societies, have become very suspicious of the idea of authority. They don't readily accept anybody's authority, whether that's the authority of a parent, school teacher, police officer or an institution (such as the Church).

In such a cynical climate, it is really important for us not to allow our minds to conform to the prevailing mood of the times but rather to be transformed by the wisdom that has outlasted the centuries and will still be inspiring billions of people long after the present age, with its sometimes anarchic rebellion against truth and authority, will have disappeared. We need to learn to be humble as well as confident. We must admit that claims for truth need to be backed up and that an assertion without qualification is not enough. At the same time we must also resolutely hold on to the fact that the Bible affords us the most intellectually coherent view of the world (as even atheists have admitted). We must also agree that human authority has sometimes been abused and that many both inside and outside the church have been wounded by those they trusted to be their fathers and mothers (literally or figuratively). This does not mean doing away with authority altogether, however. It means having our broken, fatherless hearts restored and rediscovering the loving authority of our perfect Father in heaven—one that heals and doesn't harm us.

The Hole in the Soul

In view of the claims I'll be making in this study of Biblical prophecy, I need to establish some sort of foundation or baseline. Your acceptance or otherwise of what you've read so far, and what you'll read from here on, will depend very much on your view of the authority of the Bible. This is so important that I feel it is necessary to outline briefly my understanding of this vital subject. I say "briefly" because such topics as the authority, the inerrancy, the clarity, the necessity, the sufficiency of Scripture are hotly debated by systematic theologians. Tomes have been written on the subject, or aspects of the subject, by authors defending a number of different positions. I am going to restrict myself to one chapter!

If we are to make any headway in this area we need to be up front about our assumptions from the start. Let me share mine.

My main assumption is that God exists. That is a stumbling block to many and viewed as a very real problem by some purist philosophers. The acceptance of such a supposition requires a step of faith. But can we know that God exists? I believe we all have an inner awareness; a "God shaped hole," in our being which we can fill with God's love, with a substitute for that love, or supress. The internal intuition is strengthened into confident knowledge whenever we take a step of faith and commit ourselves to Jesus.

When the living Jesus takes up residence in our hearts we then know with certainty that the Bible is God's Word. His presence in our hearts creates a self-authenticating authority when we read the Bible. We know that the Bible has authority because we have come to know the author! Author and authority are therefore intimately related. When we know the author of the Bible in our hearts then we know the authority of the Bible in our heads. We recognise the truth of the Word because we recognize the voice of the one who lives within us. As a result of getting to know Jesus, we look at the Bible from the inside outwards, as it were, and we see things very differently from when we were on the outside looking in. No longer are we looking at black printed words on a white page. We are seeing and hearing our Father's words. We are reading, in effect, a love letter from heaven.

Author and Authority

So the first way we know that God exists is through personal experience. Until we yield our lives to Christ, we have a vague intuition that He lives. We grope around in the dark, momentarily aware of the reality of God through our sense of right and wrong (our conscience) and through the innate hunger that every human being has for God—a hunger that, like physical hunger, presupposes the existence of something or, better still, someone, who can fulfil that appetite or longing.

In addition to these internal factors there are external evidences too. The world around us contains an overwhelming array of awe-inspiring realities: rain, sunshine, snowdrops, food, seasons, butterflies, water, sky, stars, flowers, trees, birds, fish and so on. All these, like the laws of nature (such as the law of gravity) are present in the universe for the purpose of supporting human beings—a fact that suggests at the very least an Intelligent Designer. Human beings themselves are the result of a remarkably complex and intricate process of breath-taking originality. Just look at the human eye—a veritable miracle of design. All these factors are surely more than the chance outcome of random currents and events. People are, like their environment, far more than human beings or some purely natural process could ever assemble. Did this all come about by accident, and for no particular purpose? I believe—along with billions of others—that such external evidences point to a Creator.

Perhaps you can admit this: while there are things we do not understand in the natural world (such as the apparently random processes by which human cells become cancerous, leading to suffering and death), there is an underlying and undeniable harmony and order in the universe. What is the cause of this intricate and complex coherence? To those who say that all this is the result of an initial singularity—the Big Bang theory—I ask what countless others ask. What came before the Singularity? What caused it? Who caused the first cause? If the universe has been ever expanding from an almost infinitesimally small burst of heat, light and energy, then who or what triggered that moment of startling creativity?

I believe the most credible answer is that God initiated the creation of the universe, the earth and indeed of us as human beings. My contention is that there is compelling evidence, both internal and external, that God exists. When you add to this the evidence of history—and especially the miraculous survival of the Jewish people, God's chosen people, mentioned in chapter 1—it is hard not to believe that God is real; that He exists. He is the author of the Bible and, as a result, the Bible is invested with a special, indeed a unique, authority.

Inspired by the Holy Spirit

It is accepted by everyone that the Bible was written over several thousand years by scores of different writers. Millions of people also believe that these writers were acting under divine guidance. While it is true that each writer's individuality shows through in their distinctive styles, it is also true that the authority of the one divine author behind their writing is plain to see whenever a person's eyes are spiritually opened through encountering Jesus. When a person meets Jesus they readily believe and endorse the Bible's claim for itself that all the words of Scripture are God's words, breathed into the writers of the Bible by the Holy Spirit (2 Timothy 3:16). These writers were peculiarly aware of this experience of special inspiration. That is why so many of them (especially the prophets of the Old Testament) exclaim, "Thus saith the Lord!" It is also why the Bible contains warnings that to disbelieve or disobey anything a Biblical prophet says is to disbelieve or disobey God. As far as the Biblical writers were concerned, they were declaring and inscribing the very words of God. That is why Jesus and the apostles regarded the Old Testament (the Hebrew Scriptures revered by faithful Jews to this day) as the authoritative Word of God. By the time the New Testament era had ended (roughly the end of the first century AD), their God-breathed words were being recognized by the Church as being the authoritative Word of God as well. Even though their voices are different—witness the difference between Mark's story of Jesus and John's—the same "author" is ultimately responsible for all their writings, which is why all their writings carry an authority beyond anything in any other book ever written.

The key to this sense of truthfulness and authority is the Holy Spirit—the Spirit of truth. The writers of the Bible were especially conscious that the one inspiring them was the Holy Spirit. They were aware when they were writing in the flow of this divine inspiration, and they were equally aware when they were transmitting their own thoughts. For example, the Apostle Paul makes it clear when he is speaking on his own authority, as in 1 Corinthians 7:12. He knows therefore that his words are his own wisdom rather than wisdom imparted by the illumination of the Spirit. At the same time Paul's words are still "trustworthy" (1 Corinthians 7:25) because they are uttered by one who was filled with the Holy Spirit and who sought always to speak 'words of wisdom' rather than the mere 'wisdom of words.'

The Biblical writers were therefore men and women who sought at all times to be faithful to the inspiration of the Holy Spirit. In John 14:26 and John 16:13 Jesus promised that the Holy Spirit would bring all that he had said to the disciples' remembrance and would guide them in all truth. This is precisely what the author of John's Gospel experienced! The Holy Spirit brought the teachings and episodes of Jesus to remembrance and gave him extraordinary, supernatural insight into the meaning and significance of Christ's words and actions. When this same Jesus is invited into a person's heart, that person knows that the words of the Bible are true because he or she knows in person the one to whom the entire Bible points and around whom the entire Bible revolves—Jesus the Messiah, the Son of God, the Word made Flesh!

This is precisely what gives a human being the sense that the Bible is true truth and that it has a loving, divine authority to guide them on all matters relating to belief and behaviour. The person who does not have the Holy Spirit sees only literary writings when they read the Bible. Theirs is a naturalist reading experience—one devoid of supernatural encounter, one deeply cynical about the truth and authority of what they are reading. However, when a person encounters the Risen Lord and invites him to live and reign within their heart, that person is no longer bound by the restrictive and reductionist worldview of the naturalist. That person has become a spiritual man, a spiritual woman, and has a supernatural mindset.

The Apostle Paul wrote this: "The natural man does not receive the things of the Spirit of God, for they are folly to him, and he is not able to understand them because they are spiritually discerned" (1 Corinthians 2:14). Jesus said: "My sheep hear my voice, and I know them, and they follow me" (John 10:27).

Do you get the picture?

You will never truly appreciate the absolute truth or the divine authority of the Bible until you come to know Jesus and find yourself filled with the same Holy Spirit who inspired the Biblical writers.

When Pilate asked, 'What is truth?' he failed to see the irony of his question. He was standing in the very presence of Truth—the one who said, "I am the way, the truth, and the life" (John 14:6). Truth is not an abstract noun. Truth is a living person. When you have this person living in your heart, you'll know the truth of the Bible! When you have the Incarnate Word, you'll know the life-changing power of the Inscribed Word. When Scripture is read with spiritual integrity, and each part is examined within both its Biblical and cultural contexts, the Bible is deemed to be historically accurate and internally consistent. It is seen to contain prophecies that have been miraculously fulfilled and which have influenced the course of history, maintaining a continuing relevance and authority over thousands of years of demographic and social change. Truly "the Word of the Lord abides forever."

Circular Arguments

Having read this, some may ask if this isn't all a circular argument in which the proof of the Bible's authority is dependent on the Bible's own statement that it is what it says it is. Isn't that circular reasoning?

Anyone who wants to think philosophically about this issue will have to end up admitting that a circular argument is all that's possible in this situation. How can you appeal to a greater authority than the Bible in proving the Bible's authority? If we do that, we have to assume that there is something that has greater authority than God because of course God is the author of the Bible. If we appeal to logic or common sense to prove the case then we have to elevate these above God as well! If God is the Supreme Being, then there is nothing higher or greater to which we can appeal, not even logic.

In the end what really convinces people that the Bible is God's Word, that it contains true truth, and that it carries divine and infallible authority, is not any argument from theology or philosophy. Rather it is experiencing Jesus that does that. The Bible (by which I mean the Old and the New Testaments together) is a Christ-centred book. It is, more accurately, an ancient library of 66 books whose authors are all inspired by the Holy Spirit to speak prophetically about Jesus. This means that logic cannot sway a person to believe that the Bible is true and authoritative. No, only love can do that. Falling in love with Jesus is the game-changing factor. Once you get to know the author of the Bible, you get to honour the authority of the Bible.

The Bible is best read and interpreted by people in love.

Are you in love with its author?

Are you in love with the one to whom all its pages lead?

Chapter 5: A GRADUAL UNVEILING

A couple of years ago I sensed the Lord saying the following to me: "Look at my servant Robert Boyle; he did not "invent" Boyle's Law, rather he discovered, by diligent study and experiment, one of my laws—one of many that provide order to the universe."

This set me reflecting about the process of unveiling—specifically the gradual way prophecy, or for that matter scientific understanding, is revealed over time, by research and/or by divine disclosure.

I knew nothing about Robert Boyle, other than a rudimentary schoolboy recollection of the principle that the volume of any gas in a container, where pressure is applied to the gas, will be inversely proportional to the amount of pressure applied. So I googled his name and discovered that as well as being a scientist, considered by some to be the founder of modern chemistry, he was also a theologian and a committed Christian. As I learned this I became convinced that scientific discovery is the gradual unveiling of God's pre-existing laws. The fundamental elements and laws of nature, from which our understanding grows, and from which men "make" things, have been there since God created them. They've been waiting for us to observe them.

The EM Spectrum

In developing this line of thought I started to consider the electromagnetic (EM) spectrum. The first awareness of the theoretical existence of EM waves has been credited to James Clerk Maxwell, working in the 1860s and 70s. His theories were applied, for more practical use, in the development of radio communications by Heinrich Hertz in the late 1880s and early 1890s. Today we are heavily dependent on a wide range of technological equipment that uses radio waves, or microwaves, infra-red, visible light, ultra-violet, x-rays or gamma-rays. Perhaps the most obvious and startling advances have been in computing and mobile telephony.

We cannot see the EM spectrum: it is, however, a dimension on which we all rely every day. Even though it is relatively new to us, it has, of course, always been there!

From my own experience in the Royal Corps of Signals I can confidently say that in military terms the EM spectrum constitutes the fourth dimension of warfare. Monitoring electronic activity, gathering and transmitting battlefield information, managing weapons systems, jamming enemy command and control capabilities, and generally dominating activity in the EM spectrum is a prime requisite to achieving advantage in any military operation.

In other words, that which 150 years ago we did not even know existed is now a fundamental part of the way we live. Most of us don't feel a need to understand how our computer works in order to use its huge capability (or a fraction of its huge capability). Neither do we have to understand electricity to switch on the light!

A Slow Unveiling

There are countless truths in the Bible which have been there since the end of the first century AD, even earlier. They have been there all along, some of them waiting "for such a time as this" before they are fully observed and then applied. When we start to access this revelation, we may know it works without necessarily understanding how or why.

This does not mean we should do away with our understanding. What it does mean is that, as the prophet Habakkuk said, "revelation awaits its appointed time." A prophecy may be given in one century but not necessarily understood or applied until many centuries later, when people with eyes to see observe that it is being fulfilled in their own time.

Take for example the prophecy of the Suffering Servant in Isaiah 53. There is a great deal of debate about when this extraordinary and extreme picture of the suffering Messiah was given to the prophet. The most probable view is that it was given during the first half of the 6th century BC, when the Jewish people were suffering the Exile in Babylon.

Six centuries later Jesus was condemned to death by the Roman governor Pontius Pilate. He was scourged and tormented by Roman legionaries and then forced to carry the crossbeam of his own instrument of death to a location outside the walls of Jerusalem, known by the haunting name 'The Place of the Skull.' There he was crucified.

Did Isaiah know that his prophetic portrait was in fact a revelation of the future Passion of the Christ?

Did the Jewish people know that the following words were going to be fulfilled in the death of a man known as Yeshua ('Jesus')?

Surely He has borne our griefs
And carried our sorrows;
Yet we esteemed Him stricken,
Smitten by God, and afflicted.
But He was wounded for our transgressions,
He was bruised for our iniquities;
The chastisement for our peace was upon Him,
And by His stripes we are healed.
All we like sheep have gone astray;
We have turned, every one, to his own way;
And the LORD has laid on Him the iniquity of us all.
He was oppressed and He was afflicted,
Yet He opened not His mouth;

He was led as a lamb to the slaughter,
And as a sheep before its shearers is silent,
So He opened not His mouth.
He was taken from prison and from judgment,
And who will declare His generation?
For He was cut off from the land of the living;
For the transgressions of My people He was stricken.
And they made His grave with the wicked—
But with the rich at His death,
Because He had done no violence,
Nor was any deceit in His mouth.

Here is a graphic example of how the significance of Biblical prophecy is not fully accessed until its fulfilment in space and time. Here a prophecy given in Babylon between 587 and 536 BC is fulfilled outside Jerusalem in approximately AD 30! There are hundreds of Biblical prophecies yet to be fulfilled concerning the Second Coming of Jesus. These have been waiting until our own times!

Furthermore these words, written some 600 years before the death of Jesus, must have been mysterious and incomprehensible to readers of the time. It is only after the events to which the words refer have taken place that the writings make sense. I believe the same sense of a need for "unveiling" can be said of the book of Revelation; the mysterious parts will come clear as events unfold.

You Need Faith

The unveiling of a Biblical prophecy not only awaits its appointed time in history, it may also await its appointed time in my own life. That is, it awaits an appropriate moment when I am ready to see what it really means and then observe its significance in relation to world events today. When that happens there is a startling process of 'defamiliarisation'. A passage in Scripture that was familiar to me now seems to be unfamiliar! It is as if I am seeing old and familiar truths in a new and unfamiliar way.

I have often had this experience. Time and again I have been surprised by a new insight or understanding of something in Scripture that I have read many times before. Something that was always there, like the EM spectrum, has been waiting the moment when I am ready to observe it.

For me, the significance of Biblical prophecy (especially those connected with the End Times) has similarities to the EM spectrum. For a time I may not see it but I know it exists and that I will understand it in due course. The early EM pioneers like Maxwell, Hertz, and their colleagues and successors, built on a vague awareness and then a growing understanding about radio waves. In like manner, we can develop our knowledge of what God has revealed in the Bible, rely on it and eagerly anticipate further enlightenment.

In all of this we cannot do without faith. Faith is the ability to believe in your heart what you cannot yet see with your eyes. Nowhere is this truer than in our relationship with Jesus. Jesus Christ died two thousand years ago. He is no longer physically present in a body on the earth. Therefore we cannot see him with our eyes. At the same time, Christians believe that Jesus Christ was raised from the dead on the third day after his crucifixion. This means that He is alive today and that we can therefore know Him in our hearts in a personal and relational way.

Think about it for a moment. Julius Caesar was once alive but now is dead for evermore. The same can be said about Caesar Augustus, Pontius Pilate, Genghis Khan, Adolf Hitler and Stalin. The same will be true before long of Richard Dawkins and other prominent atheists. But of Jesus alone can it be said that once He was dead but now He is alive for evermore!

When a person comes to faith in Christ, they begin to believe that He is real even though they cannot see Him face to face. They go on believing in Him even though they cannot see Him until one day He returns on the clouds in great glory at the climax of history. Then they will see the one in whom they believed.

All this is extremely important for understanding Biblical prophecies, especially about signs of the End Times. We cannot start to grow in our understanding until we have first put our trust in Jesus. Once we have chosen to believe in Him, then the words of the Bible become luminous to us. What was there all along becomes something we can see!

All this can be summed up in the ancient Latin motto, *credo ut intelligam*: I believe so that I may understand.

We will understand the significance of prophetic passages in the Bible only when we observe them (and current events) with the eyes of faith.

Understanding follows believing.

If you don't believe in Jesus, you won't understand the Scriptures.

If you do believe in Jesus, then you will have eyes to see and a heart to understand everything that the Bible teaches about the signs of the End Times.

If you want just one very powerful example, read on!

Chapter 6: WHERE SATAN HAS HIS THRONE

If you go on holiday to Turkey today, the chances are you may well be invited to sign up for a tour to a place called Pergamum. Pergamum was one of the cities in Asia Minor (modern Turkey) where Roman influence can be most clearly seen. Situated on a hill there is an altar to Zeus where historians and archaeologists now believe the Roman Emperor was worshipped by the citizens of the city. Every year, on the Emperor's birthday, the Caesar of the day was adored by people throughout his Empire who addressed him as 'son of god', 'saviour of the world', and 'lord.'

In the Book of Revelation, the risen and ascended Jesus dictates a letter to the Apostle John—a follower of Christ who is now a prisoner of the Romans on the penal colony of Patmos. He is in chains because he has refused to bow his knee to the Emperor. For him there is only one man in history who deserves the honorific titles 'Son of God', 'Saviour of the World,' and 'Lord.' His name is Jesus. For John the consequences of refusing to confess Caesar as Lord were severe—imprisonment on a barren rock. It was while he was incarcerated there that he saw the Ascended Jesus.

In these visions, Jesus tells John what to write to the church in Pergamum:

'These things says He who has the sharp two-edged sword: "I know your works, and where you dwell, where Satan's throne is. And you hold fast to My name, and did not deny My faith even in the days in which Antipas was My faithful martyr, who was killed among you,

where Satan dwells. But I have a few things against you, because you have there those who hold the doctrine of Balaam, who taught Balak to put a stumbling block before the children of Israel, to eat things sacrificed to idols, and to commit sexual immorality.Thus you also have those who hold the doctrine of the Nicolaitans, which thing I hate. Repent, or else I will come to you quickly and will fight against them with the sword of My mouth.

"He who has an ear, let him hear what the Spirit says to the churches. To him who overcomes I will give some of the hidden manna to eat. And I will give him a white stone, and on the stone a new name written which no one knows except him who receives it.'"

There is a great deal I could say about this passage but I want to pull out one sentence:

"I know your works, and where you dwell, where Satan's throne is."

The throne mentioned here can only refer to one thing—the temple-like structure which is known as the Pergamum Altar, built around 200BC. This temple is also mentioned by the Roman historian Tacitus (56-117AD) in his Annals, and in Plutarch's (45-120 AD) Life of Caesar. The mound on which it was situated is still visible today.

Satan's Headquarters

Pergamum was a city of considerable importance in the first century AD when the *Book of Revelation* was written. It was a thriving metropolis with a healing complex called the Asklepion, after the Greek serpent-god Asclepius. The citizens of Pergamum were known as "the Temple Keepers of Asia"; they worshiped a myriad of gods, especially Caesar.

When inhabitants of this city started to follow Jesus, this immediately put them on a collision course with the pagan and demonic systems in their locality. In particular it threw them into a conflict with the Caesar-worship, pervasive throughout the Roman Empire—a worship that gave unity to the Roman colonies throughout the globe.

From what John sees and hears it seems that from the Ascended Christ's perspective Pergamum is the location in Asia Minor where it can be safely said that "Satan has his throne" and where "Satan lives." Imagine that! You are a Christian in Pergamum and you discover when this letter is read that you have the same address as Satan!

What was it about Pergamum that justified this description? The answer is clear. This city was the seat of Emperor Worship. It was the very epicentre of idolatry. It was the prime location for the worship of the incarnation of Satan on earth—the Roman Emperor who demanded to be revered and idolised as son of god, saviour of the world, and lord.

How on earth could a Christian survive in such a city?

The answer is, 'not easily.' Every Christian who lived in this city, whose permanent address was 'Pergamum, Asia Minor,' had to make a choice. "Will I burn incense to the Roman Emperor and confess that Caesar is lord? Or will I bow the knee to Jesus and confess that Christ is Lord and Him alone?" That was a choice that could cost you everything.

And it did cost one man everything. Did you notice the part in the letter where the Ascended Christ talks about a man called Antipas? The name Antipas means "against everything." This man stood courageously against everything to do with Satan in his city. He confessed that Christ is Lord but Caesar is not. He became a "faithful martyr."

What is it about Antipas that Jesus particularly applauds? It is the fact that even in the face of an excruciating death, this man held fast to the name of Jesus. He heroically continued to give testimony to his faith that Jesus alone is the Son of God, Saviour of the World, and Lord, even when he was about to be murdered in a ritualistic sacrifice on the Pergamum Altar.

Satan Relocates his Throne

Let's now fast forward nearly 2000 years. In 1878 the German engineer and archaeologist Carl Humann started excavating the Pergamum Altar. In 1902 Kaiser Wilhelm II ordered that the whole structure, including the Gigantomachy Frieze, be transported to Berlin. The 113 metre sculptured frieze around the base of the altar depicts the struggle between the gods and the giants in Greek mythology. The altar was reconstructed, first in the Kaiser Freidrich Museum and subsequently moved to the specially built Pergamon Museum, on Museum Island. Kaiser Wilhelm II claimed this was the greatest achievement of his reign.

Image: Altar to Zeus in the Pergamonmuseum, Berlin by Lestat (Jan Mehlich) (Own work) [GFDL (http://www.gnu.org/copyleft/fdl.html), CC-BY SA-3.0 (http://creativecommons.org/licenses/by-sa/3.0/)

In 1933, Hitler was elected Chancellor of Germany and in 1934 he ordered the building of a Tribune at Zeppelin Field in Nuremberg. The architect, Albert Speer, is said to have used the Pergamum Altar as a model for the much larger scale "Zeppelintribune". It took three years to build and it was from a podium at the centre of this vast edifice that Hitler took the salute during the Nazi rallies in Nuremberg.

In 1934, Adolf Hitler commissioned a German movie star called Leni Riefenstahl to direct and film one of the huge rallies before this throne-like edifice in Nuremburg. This film shows Hitler in the most god-like of all his appearances. Known as *Triumph of the Will*, it shows Hitler descending from the heavens into the presence of his starry-eyed and adoring followers. The year after this film (the only movie ever made about Hitler), one million people came to the rally in Zeppelin Field before the replicated Pergamum Altar. The movie was shown every year for the following twelve years. It intentionally portrayed Hitler as a modern day Caesar, descending the steps of his Pergamum Altar to the acclaim of the soldiers in his twentieth century version of the Roman war machine (eagle standard and all). Truly Satan had relocated his throne.

Image: Muster of the Labour Service (RAD), Zeppelin Field, Party Congress 1937. Bundesarchiv, Bild 183-C12701 / CC-BY-SA [CC BY-SA 3.0 de (http://creativecommons.org/licenses/by-sa/3.0/de/deed.en)], via Wikimedia Commons from Wikimedia Commons

Signposts of the End

Does any of this strike you as significant? The word 'significant' contains the word 'sign.' Do you think that the Holy Spirit might be trying to teach us something from the example of Satan's throne? Do you believe that the Pergamum Altar might in some ways be a sign pointing to a deeper reality than the one available to our physical senses? Do you agree that the example of the Pergamum Altar shows how in at least some instances the significance of Biblical passages written thousands of years ago can only fully be discerned at such a time as ours? Remember the words of the Book of Daniel: *"But you, Daniel, close up and seal the words of the scroll until the time of the end"* (Daniel 12:4).

Your answers to the questions above will depend on a number of factors. It will depend on whether you believe in Jesus, whether you know the Author of the Bible and therefore respect its authority, whether you trust in God and have faith that He is the beginning and the end, the Alpha and Omega of human history.

Above all it will depend on your view of the world. If you have a naturalist worldview—a worldview that denies the existence of a supernatural realm—then the reconstruction of the Pergamum Altar at Nuremburg will either just be a coincidence or perhaps a sociological, or even a psychological, phenomenon. If you have a Christian worldview, you will not so easily be able to reduce such factors to a naturalist explanation. You will more readily believe that these are visible signs in our times that point to invisible realities and that the Nazi rallies at a Pergamum-like Altar are warning signs—signposts alerting those who have eyes to see that we have entered into the End Times prophesied in the Bible. You may even go so far as to say that the same demonic spirit that motivated the anti-Christian Roman imperialism of the first century is now influencing world leaders and events in the twentieth and twenty first centuries, causing them to unite behind Satan's Final Solution—to conduct a holocaust in which God's people are forced to make a decision between confessing Christ or Caesar as Lord.

So what is your worldview?

And what do you believe is the significance of the phrase "Satan's throne" in our own times?

Part 2: Israel and Babylon

Chapter 7: THE MIRACLE THAT IS ISRAEL

What are the odds of you being injured by a lightning strike in any given day?

The answer, apparently, is 1 in 250,000,000.

What is the probability of a meteorite landing on your house?

It's 1 in 180,000,000,000,000!

Now let me ask a different question. What is the probability of just eight of the Old Testament prophecies concerning the Messiah being fulfilled in just one man?

There are actually many more than just eight prophecies. But let's restrict ourselves to eight because a scientific study on this number was conducted a few years ago by Peter Stoner and Robert Newman in a book called Science Speaks. Their findings were endorsed by the American Scientific Affiliation. They worked out that the probability of just eight of the 60 Old Testament prophecies (with 270 further ramifications) being fulfilled in Jesus of Nazareth was … are you ready for this?

1 in 100,000,000,000,000,000!

That's astronomically low.

It is almost inconceivably low.

Here are some examples of fulfilled prophecy relating to Jesus' First Coming:

Prophecy Fulfilled	Old Testament	New Testament
Born of a virgin	Isaiah 7:14	Matthew 1:22-23
Born in Bethlehem	Micah 5:2	Luke 2:4-6
Called out of Egypt	Hosea 11:1	Matthew 2:14-15
Taught in parables	Psalms 78:1-2	Matthew 13:34-35
Healed the sick	Isaiah 29:18-19, 35:4-6, 61:1	Matthew 11:2-6
Entered Jerusalem on a donkey	Zechariah 9:9	John 12:12-15
Flogged and abused	Isaiah 50:5-6	Mark 14:53-15:20
Hands and feet pierced	Psalms 22:16	Mark 15: 20-26
Clothes divided	Psalms 22:18	Matthew 27:35
Killed and Buried	Isaiah 53:8-9	Mark 15:33-47
Rose on the third day	Hosea 6:2	1 Corinthians 15:3-4

When we look at the prophets of the Old Testament and what they predicted about the First Coming of Jesus we are in reality looking at something that a purely naturalist mind cannot understand or explain. This is supernatural. The prophets were clearly foretelling the future with the help of the Holy Spirit, not in their own strength. All the prophecies about the First Coming of Jesus have been fulfilled. That is a miracle!

But this has seismic implications for our appreciation of the many prophecies concerning the Second Coming of Jesus. If the prophecies about his First Coming have been fulfilled, we can expect that the prophecies concerning his Second Coming will be fulfilled too. Every detail surrounding the circumstances of his return contained within Biblical prophecies will come true, just as they did first time round.

The Importance of Israel

Before I go any further I want to stress something extremely important about Biblical prophecy and that is the simple fact that all the prophets were pointing to Jesus when they gave utterance to the revelation they received. The Coming of Jesus was the central theme of their predictions, whether that was his First or his Second Coming. The Biblical prophets were pointing to and magnifying Jesus when they prophesied. Anyone claiming to be a prophet today can be evaluated by the same criterion. As Revelation 19:10 says, "The testimony of Jesus is the spirit of prophecy." In other words, the key question to ask of any purported modern day prophecy is, "Does it witness to and exalt Jesus Christ, born of a virgin, crucified for our sins, raised from the dead, and today reigning in heaven as God's Only Son?"

As Hamlet once said, "that is the question."

I emphasize this because one of the key events predicted in the New Testament is the restoration of the nation of Israel. Jesus said that this would be a sign of the times. What times was he referring to? The End Times, the climax of history. The restoration of the nation of Israel and the return of the Jewish people to their ancient homeland are events prophesied in Scripture. As I argued in an earlier chapter, this was fulfilled in part in the 6th century BC when the 50,000 Jewish exiles returned to Judah from Babylon. But it began to be fully fulfilled in 1948 when the unthinkable happened: after two thousand years of displacement from their God-given land, the Jewish people were reinstated as a nation and in a single day! Israel, therefore, has a vital place in Biblical prophecy.

This does not mean, however, that Israel is more important than Jesus. The Bible does not say that the testimony of Israel is the spirit of prophecy. It says that the testimony of Jesus is! This is a critical reminder. There are people today who focus more on Israel than they do on Jesus. That is not my intention nor is it my theology. I believe that Jesus is the central theme and the supreme priority not only of genuine prophecy but of the entire Bible. My faith is Christ-centred, not Israel-centred.

At the same time, it has to be seen and cannot be denied that Jesus was born as a Jewish baby, within the history of Israel. The New Testament opens with the record of the genealogy, birth and ministry of Jesus, describing Him as "the Son of David, the son of Abraham;" (Matthew 1:1). Jesus was "a servant of the Jews on behalf of God's truth" (Romans 15:8). The angel told Mary that the son she was to bear would be King on "the throne of his father David and he will reign over the house of Jacob forever" (Luke 1:32-33). The question the Magi asked ("Where is the one who has been born king of the Jews?"—Matthew 2:2) relates to a commonly held *Jewish expectation.*

All these and countless other statements show that Jesus' birth was a critical moment within the overarching story of His nation, Israel. His story was part of Israel's history.

My belief is that His story continues to be of vital importance to the history of Israel.

A Brief History of Israel

The significance of Israel is so fundamental to our understanding of the timeline of Biblical prophecy that I need to provide a brief chart of Jewish history. Note: while many of the dates, particularly early BC, are debated, for the main part the order of events is not.

DATE	EVENT	COMMENT
C 2100 BC	Abraham and Sarah begin the journey to Judaism	Abraham, son Isaac and grandson Jacob are the "Patriarchs" or fathers of Judaism
C 1915 BC	Jacob (aka Israel) and Rachel have a son Joseph	Joseph sold into slavery in Egypt, becomes Chief Minister to Pharaoh

C 1890 BC	Famine in the land: Joseph "re-discovered" by his brothers	Jacob's family moves to Egypt
Up to C 1446 BC	Enslavement of "Children of Israel" in Egypt	Over period of 200 years guest status turns to slave status
C 1446 BC	Moses leads Hebrews out of Egypt	12 tribes of Israel occupy Canaan, after 40 years in the wilderness
C 1000 BC	King David unites and grows the kingdom	David takes over from Israel's first king, Saul
C 970 BC	King Solomon, son of David, builds first temple in Jerusalem	After his death, the country splits: Israel in north, Judah in south
C 720 BC	Assyrians destroy Israel	North. Assyrian capital Nineveh (now Mosul) destroyed c 612 BC
C 605 - 586 BC	Judah destroyed by the Babylonians	Jewish people (from Judah in the south) go into exile
C 538 – 516 BC	Second Temple built	Cyrus the Persian released the exiles
C 6-4 BC	Jesus Born	Exact date much debated!
C 30 AD	Jesus Crucified	
70 AD	Second Temple destroyed	Romans lay siege to and destroy Jerusalem
1492	Jews expelled from Spain	
1938	Holocaust begins	Nazi persecution
1945	WW2 Ends	
1948	State of Israel declared; nation reborn in a day (as prophesied)	Jews start to return to the Land from all over the world

As we have already seen, the Biblical predictions (prophecies) of a restored Israel are startling, and the re-establishment of the Jewish nation in Israel, fulfilled in 1948, is even more so. The survival of their national identity in dispersion, which the Jews maintained for nearly nineteen hundred years, prior to the rebirth of Israel, is an incredible phenomenon. I have pointed above to just one of many instances of anti-Jewish persecution between AD 70 and the Holocaust in WW2—the expulsion of the Jews from Spain. Mark Twain was right. It is quite frankly a mystery and a miracle that the Jewish people survived between AD 70 and 1948.

Why Israel Had to Survive

Why then has Israel survived? We can begin to glimpse the answer to this vital question if we look briefly at a much neglected passage in the New Testament. Most preachers who decide to give a whole series of talks on the New Testament letter known as the *Book of Romans* stop at the end of Romans chapter 8. Romans chapters 1 to 8 are full of rich revelation about what Jesus did for us when he died for our sins. Chapters 9-11, however, turn from the importance of Jesus' death and resurrection to the importance of the Jewish people from whom Jesus was born. The author, the Apostle Paul, was himself Jewish and loved the Jewish people, longing for them to see what he now saw—that Jesus was their Messiah and the Son of God. He also longed for those in his churches who were not Jewish (known as "Gentiles") to see the importance of the Jewish ancestry of Jesus and the importance of the nation of Israel in the preparation for both the First Coming and the Second Coming of Jesus.

Why is this important? Let's remember that God chose one small people group out of all the nations of the earth. He didn't choose the Egyptians with their great pyramids, or the Greeks with their great wisdom, or the Romans with their great armies. He chose a bunch of nomads, saying to one of them (Abraham) that he had chosen to give this special privilege to Israel so that Israel in turn could take God's blessing to all the nations on the earth. When Israel failed to pass on the blessings of God to the Gentile nations, God sent his one and only Son, the Messiah Jesus, to fulfil what Israel had failed to fulfil—to bring the peoples of every tribe and nation into an intimate relationship with their Father in heaven. This was why Jesus was born as a Jew in Israel—to do what Israel seemingly couldn't do, and to pay the price for both Jews and Gentiles to have access to the Father.

It is to this history and destiny that the Apostle Paul refers in Romans 9-11. Paul points out that the Jewish people are God's chosen people. They are the nation whom the Father adopted out of His great love. But this same nation also failed to fulfil its destiny—failed ultimately to even recognize Jesus, who was born as one of them, as their Messiah.

What then does this mean for Israel? What it does not mean is this: that the Father declared the adoption of Israel null and void, decreeing that his people were now no longer chosen. As far as Paul is concerned, once adopted, always adopted. God's covenants are eternal not temporal. When this Father makes a promise, He keeps it. The birth of the church therefore does not mean either that the church has replaced Israel or that Israel has been rejected. No, God's love for Israel is unending. He plans to keep His hand upon Israel until the end of history, never giving up on the nation he adopted from all those on the earth.

This is great love indeed.

It is like the love of the father in the story that Jesus told in Luke 15—a love that refused to stop loving either his younger or his older son when they failed to honour and love him as they should.

The Father will not let go of Israel, come what may. He is waiting, like the father of the prodigal, for Israel to turn around and come home into His affectionate embrace. He is waiting for the day when all Israel will be saved (Romans 11:26).

The Olive Tree

What then does all this mean for those in the church who are not Jewish by birth or descent? It stands to reason that if God hasn't finished with Israel then those who come to know Jesus and who are not Jewish must in some way or another have a part in Israel's continuing history until the day when all Israel will be saved. This is the profound mystery that Paul deals with in Romans 11. He knows that this subject is hard to grasp so he uses a word picture to aid us in our understanding. He talks about a cultivated olive tree—a very common sight in Israel, even to this day.

The gist of Paul's teaching is this: that God planted and cultivated an olive tree when He called Israel. This tree has its roots in the lives of Abraham, Isaac and Jacob—three ancient Israelites known as "the patriarchs." Many branches have grown on this cultivated tree since the days of these fathers of Judaism. Those people that continued to believe in God and were faithful remained part of the tree. Those that didn't were broken off.

Israel's unfaithfulness is the reason why Jesus came. He embodies all the Father's hopes for Israel. He is faithful to the commandments from His birth to His death. He is the first completely obedient Jewish person in history. He is the one and only person to fulfil God's high calling for Israel.

But many of Jesus' own people rejected Him. Many of His Jewish contemporaries refused to acknowledge that He was the Messiah and God's Son. Their lack of faith in Jesus caused them to be broken off the cultivated olive tree. While Israel as a nation was not rejected, individual Jews who denied that Jesus was the Messiah were regarded as lacking in the faith that, according to God, makes a person right with God.

This was bad news for them.

But it was good news for Gentile believers in Jesus. They, being wild (as opposed to cultivated) branches were grafted in to the olive tree, whose roots go back to Abraham, Isaac and Jacob. Gentile believers in Jesus were incorporated into the olive tree that is Israel's history and also became favoured recipients of the promises that God long ago gave to Abraham. They became the adopted children of the living God!

But here we must listen to Paul's word of warning. The incorporation of Gentile believers in Jesus does not mean that a church made up of Gentile Christians has replaced the nation of Israel. The first followers of Jesus were in any case Jewish (showing that some did believe, though not all) so that would make no sense at all. In addition, we must never forget that the Father hasn't given up on Israel, never will.

This means that we cannot and should not embrace what has been called 'replacement theology'—the view that the New Testament teaches that the church (understood as a principally Gentile Christian church) has replaced Israel in God's affections and plans.

No, Gentile believers in Jesus are wild olive branches that have been grafted into the cultivated olive tree—a tree made up of faith-filled Israelites since the time of Abraham. We are now a part of faithful Israel's story. Indeed, we cannot and must not separate ourselves from that story.

An End Times Harvest

From a reading of the New Testament as a whole it seems that one thing is clear: that from the time of the Apostle Paul's ministry onwards, a time of grace was extended to those outside the nation of Israel, in other words to Gentiles. This time of grace was a timeframe in which Gentiles could hear and respond to the Good News about Jesus and come to enjoy the blessings of the promises given to Israel, not least the promise of the gift of the Holy Spirit. The very fact that in the first century AD there was a court reserved in the Father's house (the Temple) for the Gentiles is visible confirmation that God had always intended for non-Jews to be part of His family. The fact that Jesus was furious enough to drive out the money-changers from this part of the Temple confirms that He was passionate about fulfilling Israel's destiny, to carry the blessing of the Father's love to all nations.

Does this then mean that there will never again be a season of grace for the Jews? The answer is supplied in Romans 11. The Apostle Paul makes it clear that there will come a day when the cultivated or natural branches (i.e. faithful Jewish people) will be grafted in once again—in other words, when Jewish people will start believing in Jesus on a wide scale. Indeed, Paul warns those of us who are Gentile Christians to be on our guard. If God once made room for wild branches to be grafted in by breaking off some of the natural branches, how much more will He one day make room for the natural branches by breaking off the wild branches that prove to be unfaithful to Jesus! In other words, Paul envisages a day when there is a reversal of the trends:

1st century: unfaithful Jews removed from the tree and faithful Gentiles added

21st (?) century: unfaithful Gentiles removed and faithful Jews added

Paul speaks about a time when the Jewish people—his own people—will no longer be blinded by their unbelief about Jesus. In vast numbers they will see the Deliverer from Zion (i.e. Jesus). The veil will be lifted from their understanding and they will see that Jesus of Nazareth is their Messiah and God's Son. As Paul prophesies in Romans 11:26: "All Israel will be saved." Jews will come to believe in Jesus in such numbers that we will be able to say that the nation of Israel as a whole has been saved.

The hardening of hearts against Jesus that we see in Jewish history right up to this day is therefore not a permanent one. Paul was a Jew—an extremely zealous Jew—who had come to believe in Jesus as a direct result of an encounter with the Risen Lord in a vision on the Damascus Road. He knew from his own experience that it was possible for a hard heart to turn to a soft one, for a heart of stone to be made into a heart of flesh. He knew that a Jewish man or woman could cease hostilities against Christ and his followers and come to faith in Jesus as the Messiah and Son of God. In his ministry he preached primarily to the Gentiles because this is what

God called him to do and because it was the timeframe for Gentiles to hear the Gospel and believe. But Paul never considered himself as having ceased to be a Jew, nor as having converted into a new religion, nor did he ever disparage his Jewish pedigree. Paul stated that the ultimate motivation of his ministry was the salvation of his fellow Jews (Romans 10:1).

So, to summarise: there is a timeframe in which (a) the Gospel is preached primarily to those who are not Jewish "until the full number of the Gentiles has come in"—in other words, until the number of non-Jews who confess Jesus as Lord is complete. The exact number and date of this is known only in heaven. These Gentile believers in Jesus are the wild branches of the olive tree in Romans 11. (b) Until that time, there is a remnant of faithful Jews who are chosen by grace (Romans 11:5); these are Jewish people who have chosen, like Paul, to confess that Jesus is Messiah and Lord. These are the cultivated or natural branches of the olive tree in Romans 11 because they have not had to be engrafted. When the full number of Gentile branches has come in to the olive tree, there will be a new timeframe—one in which Jewish people will turn from godlessness and look upon the one whom they pierced at Calvary and weep with repentance. There will be a great move of the Holy Spirit among the Jewish people—so great that we will be able to declare, in the midst of heartfelt adoration of God, that "all Israel is saved!"

At the very least this points to an End Times harvest in which not only are millions of Jews gathered in to the nation of Israel (in fulfilment of Scripture) but also gathered into the Kingdom of God.

The Devil's Rage

Perhaps you can see why the Jewish people had to survive against all the odds. In spite of being exiled from the Land that was promised to them by Almighty God, in spite of expulsions from other alien lands that they inhabited thereafter, in spite of periods of intense and violent persecution in many different places and times, in spite of the Final Solution (Hitler's attempt to obliterate them altogether from the face of the earth), the Jewish people have survived! Even after the appalling, demonic onslaught of the Holocaust—arguably the most evil programme ever witnessed in human history—the Jewish people somehow endured, despite losing over 6 million of their own people, 1.2 million of them children. Most miraculous of all, three years after the end of the Holocaust, part of the Promised Land was restored to the Jewish people, Israel was revived as a nation, and many Jews returned from the Diaspora to Jerusalem, the city of David.

By any standards, that is miraculous.

Over the course of the last two thousand years, since the destruction of the Temple and the sacking of Jerusalem in AD 70, the Jewish people have been subjected to a sustained attempt by the forces of hell to wipe them out. How have they managed to survive? The answer is simple. The Father has kept a chosen remnant from AD 70 until AD 1948 because He has known all along that there would come a time when the full number of Gentile believers would have come in and it would then be time, prior to the Second Coming of His Son, to bring about a great awakening of faith in Jesus in the nation of Israel. The devil has also known this all along. It is prophesied in the Scriptures and even he knows and quotes the Scriptures, when it's to his advantage. He has been desperate to prevent or postpone the establishment of appropriate (prophesied) conditions for the Second Coming. He unleashed a Slaughter of the Innocents prior to Christ's First Coming and It seems clear that he continues to try to thwart God's plan.

How it must pain him that the Jewish people survived the Final Solution. How he must have wailed when Israel was restored as a nation in 1948. And above all, how he must be howling today as more and more Jewish people, even in the land of Israel, are coming to a saving faith in Jesus.

His days are truly numbered.

Meanwhile, the natural branches on the olive tree are starting to grow and bud again!

Chapter 8: A BLOSSOMING FIG TREE

It is a curious thing that Israel, a country no larger in land mass than Wales, occupies so much attention from the global media and attracts so much activity by the world's leading politicians. Israel is a tiny nation in terms of both population and geography. Barely a week goes by without Israel being in the news headlines for one reason or another. It must strike even the most unbelieving mind as strange that the nation that is uniquely referred to in the Bible as "God's chosen people" has not only outlived all the far more powerful Empires that have come and gone but also forms such a magnetic draw to journalists and politicians alike in our own times. Isn't it at very least strange that Israel has endured the ravages of some of the most evil enemies and that it so clearly "punches above its weight" on the global stage?

In the last chapter I gave at least two reasons for this.

The first had to do with Israel's history. In Israel's past, God selected the Israelites from all the peoples of the earth and set His affections on them in a unique way. No other nation enjoys this privilege. God is a loving Father who adopted Israel. As a sign of that he gave them His Spirit (in the form of His divine presence, known as His *shekinah* glory). God is at pains to say this throughout the Old Testament (see, for example, Isaiah 51:16) and Paul makes it very clear in the chapters we have looked at (Romans 9-11). In Romans 9:4 he speaks about his own people, the Jews, and declares: "Theirs is the adoption to sonship; theirs the divine glory; the covenants; the receiving of the law, the temple worship and the promises. Theirs are the patriarchs and from them is traced the human ancestry of the Messiah, who is God over all, forever praised! Amen!"

From the perspective of history, the reason why the world is so focused on this minuscule country in the Middle East is simple: God Almighty established an everlasting covenant with Abraham and made certain promises to him, in Genesis 12, that He intends to keep. Israel—understood as those throughout history who have remained faithful to Him—will inherit these promises in the future. They will be saved (Romans 11:26).

That brings me to the second reason which has to do with Israel's destiny. When Paul speaks about Israel he does not mean every Jewish person. After all, not every Jew believes in God. In fact, if you go to the Middle East, you'll discover that Israel is paradoxically one of the most secular nations on the planet. Israel in Paul's mind does not mean every person on the earth who is ethnically speaking a Jew. It means every Jewish person who is faithful to God—who has God at the centre of their lives and exercises faith in God, come what may. As Paul puts it in Romans 9:6: "Not all who are descended from Israel are Israel." In other words, a Jewish person must be a believer in God to be regarded as a part of Israel. Jewish descent is not enough. Jewish descent plus faith in God is what not only constitutes true citizenship in Israel but also being right with God.

Now all this is admittedly challenging for our understanding and it requires not only great depths of thought but also great openness to the enlightening work of the Holy Spirit. To those who have eyes to see and a heart to understand the picture is clear. Israel has survived thus far and occupies such attention not only because of its past history (its adoption by God) but also because of its future destiny. At some point in the future, Israel is going to play a critical part in the events surrounding the return of Christ. Just as the First Coming of Christ occurred within Israel's story, so will His

Second Coming. The two cannot be separated.

What then should we be looking for in particular in Israel today?

From Olives to Figs

To answer that question we need to think about fig trees.

You would be completely justified at this point to make the complaint that I am mixing my metaphors! In the last chapter we looked at olive trees. Now I want us to look at fig trees. The reason this is so important is because of something Jesus said to his disciples in perhaps the most detailed teaching he ever gave on the signs of the End Times. I am referring to chapters 24-25 of Matthew's Gospel. There he described in the same teaching the signs that would accompany the destruction of Jerusalem forty years later (in AD 70) and the signs that would accompany the end of the world and His return.

There are many signs that Jesus alludes to that are in fact characteristic of both events. As I wrote in a previous chapter, Biblical prophecy often has both an immediate and an ultimate focus. This telescoping of short-term and long-term signs is one of the factors that make Biblical prophecies so profound. We cannot simply look at what they meant in their original setting because that would restrict us to only considering their shorter-term fulfilment. We also need to look at their longer-term significance—to their ultimate fulfilment in the events of the End Times.

This is not the time to run through every single one of the signs that accompany both the destruction of Jerusalem by the Romans in the first century and the end of all things in the future. But notice one prophecy that Jesus makes that is filled with metaphorical language. I am referring to verse 32 of Matthew 24: "Now learn this lesson from the fig tree: as soon as its twigs get tender and its leaves come out, you know that summer is near." In other words, when you see the fig tree beginning to bloom, then you will know that the return of Christ is imminent.

To understand what Jesus meant here we need to remember what I wrote in chapter 2 about the language of Biblical prophecy. Sometimes it is meant to be taken literally. At other times it must be interpreted figuratively. Now clearly Jesus is speaking metaphorically in this instance. He is not asking his followers to become horticultural experts and to observe a literal fig tree in their garden. He is speaking metaphorically. What then does the fig tree stand for? The answer is that it stands for Israel. The fig tree is a symbol used by the Old Testament prophets for Israel (Hosea 9:10; Jeremiah 24:5).

All this provides a key to interpreting what Jesus meant in Matthew 24:32. When Israel begins to blossom, then that is a clue that the return of Jesus is drawing near. Just as the blossoming fig trees in Israel indicate every year that summer is near, so when Israel is in bloom we will know that the Son is truly about to return. When the twigs are tender and the leaves have appeared, then the time is very close. The critical sign will be the fact that the fig tree is in full bloom. What then did Jesus mean by that?

The Faithful Few

To answer this question we need to remember what I wrote earlier about Paul's use of the word "Israel." In Romans 9 he makes it clear that it is not enough for a Jewish person to say that they are a citizen of Israel purely on the basis of their descent from a Jewish family. In his view, being a Jew and earning the right to be part of Israel requires that you are both Jewish by descent and a believer in God. That is certainly true if you were a Jew prior to the First Coming of Christ. However, that occurred two thousand years ago. We now know about Jesus Christ. Indeed, He is by far and away the most important person in history as can be seen by the fact that much of the world still divides history into what happened before Him and what happened after Him. He is God's only Son, the Second Person of the Trinity. That being the case, Paul requires more than simply faith in God for a Jew to be a part of Israel. Now, to be part of the chosen remnant of Israel, a Jew must also believe that Jesus is the Messiah of Israel and the Lord of lords.

In the early years of the church, in the heady days after the outpouring of the Holy Spirit at Pentecost, those who believed in Jesus were predominantly Jewish. They were based in the church in Jerusalem and they continued to live in a way that was recognizably and culturally Jewish. For example, they worshipped in the synagogues during the Sabbath (Friday sun down till Saturday sun down). The difference was that they did something else too. Unlike those Jews who worshipped on Friday and Saturday, believing in God but not in Jesus, these Jewish believers got up early Sunday morning and gathered together to worship Jesus. Why did they go this extra mile? It was because they believed that Jesus is alive because he was raised from the dead early on a Sunday morning. In their hearts, believing in God now not only meant believing that God is one (a view known as monotheism). It meant believing that God is three persons but one being (the Trinity). They assembled to worship on Sunday morning because they believed that Jesus is God.

Remember the quotation from Romans 9:4-5 earlier? Paul says Jesus is the Messiah, adding "who is God over all!"

Now that was a radical thing for a Jewish man to say.

The reason why it was radical was simple: the Jews have always insisted that God is one. They regularly recite something called the Shema Y'Israel, meaning "Hear, O Israel." This is a declaration from Deuteronomy 6: "Hear O Israel, the Lord our God, the Lord is one." For the earliest Christians like Paul to call Jesus "God" was radical. It meant that they no longer believed that God was one person. They believed that he was three—the Father, the Son, and the Holy Spirit. Yes they qualified this by saying that God is three persons but one being. But they still aroused the anger of their fellow non-Christian Jews because they were heard saying what Jesus himself had said—that He and the Father are one (John 10:30).

It should come as no surprise that relationships between Jews who did not believe in Jesus and those who did became terminally strained. While the two kinds of Jew worshipped together for a while in the early years of the church, by the turn of the century Jews who did not believe in Jesus had had enough. They were now no longer based in Jerusalem but dispersed in different lands, thanks to the sacking of Jerusalem by the Romans in AD70. By the late 80s it had become imperative that there should be no elements in the synagogues of the dispersion that would in any way threaten the purity of Judaism, or so said the ruling Pharisees based in a place called Jamnia. The first pollutants to be addressed were Jews who believed in Jesus of Nazareth.

From the end of the first century AD, there was a parting of the ways. Jews who believed in Jesus became a tiny minority, ostracised from their families and communities, denied any access to their synagogues, and in some cases even martyred for their faith in Jesus.

If it was a miracle that Israel as a nation survived, it is an even greater miracle that Israel in the sense understood by Paul (Jews who believe in Jesus) survived.

The fact is there have been precious few Jews who have seen who Jesus really is and who have been prepared to confess him as their Messiah and Lord.

The branches of the fig tree had very little fruit for two thousand years.

Until now, that is.

The Blossoming Begins

With the restoration of the nation state of Israel in 1948 everything began to change.

When the Jewish people started to return to their homeland in 1948 the records show that only twelve Jews who believed in Jesus could be counted among them.

By 1987 there were 3000 and by 1997 5000.

Today, approximate and conservative estimates indicate that there are over 20000 Jewish believers in Jesus within the borders of Israel and over 150 congregations, made up principally of Israelis who have found Jesus to be their Messiah and the Son of God.

Although this may seem a relatively small number within the context of the seven million Israelis in Israel, the numerical growth within these existing congregations, and the establishment of new congregations, has been startling over the last ten years. Something is going on in Israel. Even the Israeli press and TV networks are noticing it, portraying these Jesus-followers in a neutral and sometimes even in a positive light.

One of the reasons why these believers are being looked on favourably is because they have refused to call themselves "Christians." This is a word loaded with negative connotations within Judaism. "Christian" historically has denoted Gentile followers of Christ, some of whom have been responsible for appalling and violent acts of anti-Semitic, racial hatred. The new Israeli believers who follow Jesus do not want to have any association with that history or that mentality. They regard themselves as true Jews, celebrating the Sabbath, circumcising their children, observing the Lord's feasts, speaking Hebrew, and so forth. They play a full part in their society as Israelis, including serving in the army.

Within Israel therefore there is a significant presence of Messianic Jews who worship Yeshua (Jesus) and who are growing exponentially in number, both individually and in congregation. They are part of a global movement of Messianic Judaism that is also growing. Currently it is estimated that there are something in the order of 300,000 Messianic Jews worldwide. Jewish people everywhere are beginning to confess Jesus as Messiah and Lord.

There is clearly something going on in Israel and within the global Jewish community. In spite of opposition from many Orthodox Rabbis, Messianic Jews are growing in number and in favour. There are even stories of Orthodox Rabbis in Jerusalem beginning to see that Jesus is ha mashiach (the Messiah).

A Measurable Sign

One final comment is worth noting. When you look at Matthew 24 and the signs of both the destruction of the Temple (AD 70) and the signs of the End Times (both of which are described in that chapter), you have to admit that some of them can be witnessed in pretty well every generation. For example, Christians have been persecuted in every generation. There have been earthquakes in every generation. When we look at the world today, it is tempting to say that these things are greatly on the increase. But is that because they really are increasing? Or is it because we are much better able to know about them because of the lightning speed of communication in our media-connected global village? And even if it could be proven that they are increasing dramatically, how would we know when they had arrived at the point that Jesus talked about in Matthew 24?

I am not trying in any way to be cynical. My point is in fact the opposite. It is simply to say that when you look at the sign mentioned by Jesus, the blossoming fig tree, and interpret it within a Jewish context from a Jewish perspective, then there is a much greater probability of accuracy as far as determining the time and season is concerned. From a Jewish vantage point, and especially a Messianic Jewish one, the tender branches and the burgeoning leaves of the fig tree can only mean one thing: the miraculous softening of Jewish hearts and the burgeoning growth and life of Messianic Jewish believers in Israel and in Judaism worldwide. This is something concrete, visible and measurable. However hard it is to gain a completely scientific (accurate) record of the numbers, the growth in Messianic Judaism since 1948 is both unmistakable and remarkable.

Is it of any significance that the fig tree is blossoming again for the first time since the earliest days of the church?

Is it a sign that the summer is approaching when the Son will reappear and every eye will see him?

Is it a clue that it will not be long before Jesus returns to Jerusalem, the epicentre of the world's attention?

Is it a hint that Jesus is coming back to the very Land He left two thousand years ago?

Chapter 9: BY THE RIVERS OF BABYLON

If you've ever listened to any Reggae music you'll have heard references to "Babylon." Bob Marley produced a hit single entitled "By the Rivers of Babylon" in the early 1970s, popularised in a new cover version by Boney M in 1978. Others in the same musical tradition have made many references to "Babylon" in their lyrics.

What is the story behind this? The answer is that Bob Marley and others were alluding to the Bible and in particular to the place where the Jewish people found themselves exiled in the 6th century BC, far from their homeland. There, according to Psalm 139, the exiles sat down and wept beside Babylon's rivers.

From the Exile onwards, Babylon in the Bible symbolizes a system that enslaves people. In Reggae music it is code for any culture that oppresses its citizens. So when Bob Marley and others used Babylon in their lyrics they were setting up an analogy: every system that oppresses the African man, woman or child is like the Babylonian system that oppressed the people of Israel. For the African or Caribbean American this began with the transatlantic slave trade in which Africans were shipped in shackles to become slaves in the United States. But this isn't the end of the comparison. Babylon in Reggae music stands for any social system that enslaves people, including systems such as the global market and globalization itself.

As we will see in this chapter, Babylon hasn't just resurfaced in popular music. It is also re-emerging in covert ways in global politics.

Before we look at this sign of the End Times, however, we must refresh our memories about what the Bible says about Babylon.

Back to the Bible

The story of Babylon is interwoven in the timeline of Scripture. In this chapter I want to highlight some aspects of Babylonian history, as a base line for comment about some strange and disturbing symbolism on the global stage today that will be reviewed in the next chapter.

Babylon is first mentioned in Genesis 10, a chapter that is sometimes referred to as "the table of nations" because it lists the countries founded by the descendants of Noah, after the flood.

Noah's great grandson Nimrod, "a mighty warrior on the earth", established a kingdom in Shinar that included Babylon (synonymous with Babel) as one of its centres. Shinar is thought to have been an area between the rivers Tigris and Euphrates in what is now Iraq, formerly Mesopotamia. Babylon was on the Euphrates, located about 55 miles south of modern day Baghdad.

The first event of note concerning Babylon, recorded in Genesis 11, is the building of the Tower of Babel, which most scholars agree was a ziggurat, a many tiered structure with ramps leading upwards from each level to the next.

It seems that the people of Babylon were building the tower as a symbol of their own greatness. It was a statement of identity, self-worth and pride: it was not built to honour God.

The Bible records that God stopped the building, the builders were dispersed and the common and only language spoken by the world's population became many languages.

Genesis11 is foundational in establishing Babylon as a picture of a city of rebellion against God. From then on, references in the Bible indicate that Babylon is symbolic of sin, depravity, and defiance (e.g.1 Peter 5:13; Revelation 17.5).

Tower of Babel by Pieter Brueghel, painted in 1563

Image: Pieter Brueghel the Elder (1526/1530–1569) [Public domain], via Wikimedia Commons

Perhaps no one expressed the origins of Babylon more eloquently than Josephus, a Jewish historian in the first century (an exact contemporary with some of the New Testament authors). He describes the extraordinary pride of the ruler called Nimrod who inspired the people of his city to build something that clearly sought to dethrone God:

> *Now it was Nimrod who excited them to such an affront and contempt of God. He was the grandson of Ham, the son of Noah, a bold man, and of great strength of hand. He persuaded them not to ascribe it to God, as if it were through his means they were happy, but to believe that it was their own courage which procured that happiness. He also gradually changed the government into tyranny, seeing no other way of turning men from the fear of God, but to bring them into a constant dependence on his power... Now the multitude were very ready to follow the determination*

of Nimrod and to esteem it a piece of cowardice to submit to God; and they built a tower, neither sparing any pains, nor being in any degree negligent about the work: and, by reason of the multitude of hands employed in it, it grew very high, sooner than any one could expect; but the thickness of it was so great, and it was so strongly built, that thereby its great height seemed, upon the view, to be less than it really was. It was built of burnt brick, cemented together with mortar, made of bitumen that it might not be liable to admit water. When God saw that they acted so madly, he did not resolve to destroy them utterly, since they were not grown wiser by the destruction of the former sinners [in the Flood]; but he caused a tumult among them, by producing in them diverse languages, and causing that, through the multitude of those languages, they should not be able to understand one another. The place wherein they built the tower is now called Babylon, because of the confusion of that language which they readily understood before; for the Hebrews mean by the word Babel, confusion.

(From The Antiquities of the Jews, by the Jewish-Roman historian Josephus, c. AD 94).

The Rise of Nebuchadnezzar

By c 1900 BC, Babylon was developing as an independent city-state ruled by an Amorite dynasty. The Amorites were an indigenous Syrian race: the sixth and most famous king of this first Babylonian dynasty was Hammurabi (c 1792-1750 BC), noted for promulgating what many consider to be the first code of law in human history. Certainly, they are the most comprehensive surviving recorded set of laws. Hammurabi expanded the kingdom to form the nation-state of Babylonia. Over the next 900 years there were changing allegiances and alliances as the struggle for supremacy moved back and forth between Babylonia, the Elamite Empire, Egypt, and Assyria.

By 851 BC Babylon was independent in name only, being "protected" by its submission to Assyria.

In 745 BC Tiglath-Pileser III seized power in Assyria. He went on to conquer and subjugate most of the known world of that time. Later in his reign he was crowned king of Babylon (Babylonia).

By 625 BC Assyrian domination had declined to such an extent that a local Chaldean governor, Nabopolasser, was able to seize power and become king of Babylon.

His son and heir, Nebuchadnezzar II (who reigned from 605-561 BC), expanded the kingdom into a formidable imperial power. Nebuchadnezzar undertook a vast program of rebuilding and fortification in Babylon. Nebuchadnezzar II's glory and absolute authority surpassed that of all previous kings (and some argue, all subsequent kings). Nebuchadnezzar tightened his grip on the countries that owed allegiance to Babylon, including Judah, with Jerusalem at its centre.

After King Solomon's reign (c 970-931 BC) Israel had split into the northern kingdom of Israel and the southern kingdom of Judah. By Nebuchadnezzar's time, Judah was all that was left. Nebuchadnezzar forced King Jehoiakim of Judah to pay homage as a vassal, but Jehoiakim subsequently rebelled. Nebuchadnezzar invaded and captured Jerusalem (597 BC) and took the king, his family and other leading dignitaries to Babylon as prisoners (see 2 Kings 24).

Some scholars take this deportation in 597 BC as the beginning of the 70 year Exile of the Jews to Babylonia, as foretold by the prophet Jeremiah (Jeremiah 29:10), written sometime between c 627-586 BC.

Nebuchadnezzar appointed Zedekiah ruler of Judah. After about ten years, Zedekiah, against the advice of the prophet Jeremiah, stopped paying tribute to Babylon. He believed wrongly that Egypt would come to his aid in any confrontation with Babylon. Nebuchadnezzar returned to Jerusalem in c 587 BC, burned the city, destroyed the temple and took the remainder of the Jews captive (see Jeremiah 52).

Some scholars take this deportation in 587-6 BC as the start date of the 70 years Exile, with the completion of the rebuild of the Temple in Jerusalem in 516 BC as the end date.

Still others suggest that "70 years" is used figuratively, to represent a generation or lifetime, and others that the Scriptures are referring to the length of the Babylonian Empire, c 609 BC to c 539 BC. We will look at this in more detail later in chapter 11.

The End of the Exile

We have considered Nebuchadnezzar's determination in dealing with Judean rebellion. The prophets Daniel and Ezekiel were both deported from Jerusalem to Babylon during this period. Daniel became a leading dignitary and royal advisor to Babylonian and Persian rulers. The Book of Daniel records his famous interpretation of Nebuchadnezzar's dream (Daniel 2) while Daniel 5 shows that the writing was on the wall, literally, for Belshazzar, Nebuchadnezzar's son and successor. It foretells the fall of Babylon to the Medes and Persians. The prophet Isaiah also predicted the fall of Babylon, approximately 100 years before the event and, more startlingly, that the name of the conqueror would be Cyrus.

Cyrus II, King of Persia, captured Babylon in 539 BC, with very little resistance. It is recorded that his troops entered the city by diverting the Euphrates River into a basin dug by his engineers, so allowing them to wade into the city and surprise the garrison.

The rule of Cyrus was relatively benign. Under the Persians, Babylon retained most of its institutions and became capital of the richest satrapy in the Empire (satrap was the term used for a provincial governor in the Persian Empire). The Greek historian Herodotus described Babylon as the world's most splendid city.

Shortly after his conquest, Cyrus issued an edict:

"This is what Cyrus king of Persia says:

'The LORD, the God of heaven, has given me all the kingdoms of the earth and he has appointed me to build a temple for him at

Jerusalem in Judah. Any of his people among you may go up to Jerusalem in Judah and build the temple of the LORD, the God of Israel, the God who is in Jerusalem, and may their God be with them. And in any locality where survivors may now be living, the people are to provide them with silver and gold, with goods and livestock, and with freewill offerings for the temple of God in Jerusalem.'"

(Ezra 1:2-4 see also Ezra 6:2-5).

There are several very surprising elements to this statement. Not only were captives being released to return home, a remarkable precedent in that day and age, but Cyrus also acknowledges that Jehovah is the God of heaven and that the kingdoms that Cyrus now rules were given to him by God. Furthermore, he directs that a temple is to be built in Jerusalem, with the costs being met by the Persian people.

That is amazing!

In 1879 an explorer, Hormuzd Rassam, discovered a carved stone cylindrical "chronicle", during an excavation in Babylon. The cylinder records Cyrus' policy of returning captives and their religious treasures to their homelands. The text reads as follows:

"I returned to these sacred cities on the other side of the Tigris, the sanctuaries of which have been ruins for a long time, the images which [used] to live therein and established for them permanent sanctuaries. I [also] gathered all their [former] inhabitants and returned [them to] their habitations."

(Quoted in *The Ancient Near East: An Anthology of Texts and Pictures*. Pritchard, James B, 1973, p. 208).

This is taken from the Cyrus Cylinder, which confirms that Cyrus allowed captives to return to their homelands, and which earned him a place of honour in Jewish history. It is now in the British Museum.

Flavius Josephus, the Jewish-Roman historian (first century

AD), wrote of these events in his annals:

1. *In the first year of the reign of Cyrus which was the seventieth from the day that our people were removed out of their own land into Babylon, God commiserated the captivity and calamity of these poor people, according as he had foretold to them by Jeremiah the prophet, before the destruction of the city, that after they had served Nebuchadnezzar and his posterity, and after they had undergone that servitude seventy years, he would restore them again to the land of their fathers, and they should build their temple, and enjoy their ancient prosperity. And these things God did afford them; for he stirred up the mind of Cyrus, and made him write this throughout all Asia: "Thus saith Cyrus the king: Since God Almighty hath appointed me to be king of the habitable earth, I believe that he is that God which the nation of the Israelites worship; for indeed he foretold my name by the prophets, and that I should build him a house at Jerusalem, in the country of Judea."*

Image: By Prioryman (Own work) [CC BY-SA 3.0 (http://creativecommons.org/licenses/by-sa/3.0) or GFDL (http://www.gnu.org/copyleft/fdl.html)], via Wikimedia Commons

2. *This was known to Cyrus by his reading the book which Isaiah left behind him of his prophecies; for this prophet said that God had spoken thus to him in a secret vision: "My will is, that*

> *Cyrus, whom I have appointed to be king over many and great nations, send back my people to their own land, and build my temple." This was foretold by Isaiah one hundred and forty years before the temple was demolished. Accordingly, when Cyrus read this, and admired the Divine power, an earnest desire and ambition seized upon him to fulfil what was so written; so he called for the most eminent Jews that were in Babylon, and said to them, that he gave them leave to go back to their own country, and to rebuild their city Jerusalem, and the temple of God, for that he would be their assistant, and that he would write to the rulers and governors that were in the neighbourhood of their country of Judea, that they should contribute to them gold and silver for the building of the temple, and besides that, beasts for their sacrifices. (The Antiquities of the Jews, Book 11, Ch 1)*

Cyrus' generosity signalled the end of the Exile. The Jews returned to Jerusalem, under the leadership of Zerubbabel, in c 538 BC.

The Decline of Babylon

I want to bring this short historical overview to a close by briefly summarising aspects of the decline of Babylon.

After the time of Cyrus, there were various revolts and conquests which are summarised below:

1. **The Persian Empire.** Darius, king of Persia 522-486, recaptured Babylon, after a revolt and two year siege, in 520 BC. In the process, much damage was done, including the destruction of one hundred of the city gates. In 482 BC the Babylonians were again in rebellion and the city was ransacked, this time by Xerxes (who reigned 485-465 BC). Xerxes, who married Esther, chose to live in Susa and the significance of Babylon diminished. The Book of Esther provides information about the circumstances that were necessary for the survival of the Jews in Persia. Under subsequent Persian kings Babylon was briefly restored in

part, but never achieved its former glory.

2. **The Greek Empire.** Alexander the Great (who ruled Persia 330-323 BC and was king of Macedonia, Pharaoh of Egypt, king of Asia) started restoring Babylon but the project was abandoned after his death. He was living in Nebuchadnezzar's restored palace when he died. Alexander's generals carved up the empire and Seleucus took Babylonia, but established Seleucia, ninety miles north of Babylon, as his capital. The new city was "colonised" by people from Babylon.
3. **The Parthian Empire.** Between 160 and 140 BC Babylon was overrun by rival armies four or five times. The Parthian king Mithridates I captured the city c 140 BC, which ended the period of Greek rule. The city then fell to Antiochus VII (130 BC), to Hyspaosines (127-126 BC), before being burned and sacked by Himeros (126-123 BC). In 122 BC Mithridates II recaptured the remains of the city.

This summary of the years of decline after Cyrus is given for completeness and to provide some examples of the continuous upheavals that culminated in the virtual disappearance of the once great city of Babylon. The Bible refers to the fall of Babylon (Isaiah 13): it could be argued that Babylon had fallen at least eighteen times by c 10 BC! From that time on there are no significant records or information concerning Babylon.

There is much conflicting opinion amongst scholars on whether the Biblical prophecy about the fall of Babylon is real or metaphorical, fulfilled (past) or still to happen (future). If it is real and future, we can expect to see the city rebuilt, before the "fall" prophesied in Isaiah 21:9, Jeremiah 51:37 and Revelation 14:8 can be fulfilled.

Before we consider that further, I want to look at some more signs that come from Babylonian history which may have spiritual connotations. I hope you will be as intrigued as I am.

Chapter 10: THE TOWER AND THE GATE

Continuing our exploration of signs that may have spiritual significance, I want to consider some symbolism from the historic overview of Babylon in the previous chapter.

The Tower of Babel

Apart from signposting the pitfalls of pride and idolatry, what significance does the Tower of Babel have today? It may shock you to learn that the European Union Parliament building in Strasbourg is modelled on the unfinished Tower of Babel, as depicted in a painting by Brueghel (see poster image comparison on page 94). Here is a photograph of the EU Parliament building in Strasbourg:

Below is an architectural model of this same building:

Now take a look at the picture below:

The picture on the right was an early EU poster which, after considerable protest, was dropped. But the picture had done the damage. It had divulged the secret of the inspiration for the design of the EU building. There seems little doubt that the EU parliament building was modelled on Breughel's painting of the Tower of Babel (seen on the left).

More controversial are suggestions that the inverted star symbols represent satanic inverted pentagrams.

Doesn't it seem strange that anyone would choose to model the EU Parliament building on a tower built in defiance of God?

Is it deliberate, coincidental, or a sign—a sign not only of the re-emergence of Babylon on the world stage but a sign also of the End Times?

To help answer that question we need to look at another piece of architecture from Babylonian history, known as the Ishtar Gate.

The Ishtar Gate

Moving back to the time of Nebuchadnezzar II, I want to briefly consider a magnificent monumental structure that was built by order of the King in c 575 BC: the Ishtar Gate and Processional Way. The photograph below is of a section of the gate and processional route in the Pergamon Museum. It should be noted that the Ishtar Gate, as reconstructed here, is only the front section of the huge double gate.

Image: By Rictor Norton [CC BY 2.0 (http://creativecommons.org/licenses/by/2.0)], via Wikimedia Commons

The processional way and the Ishtar Gate formed the main and ceremonial entry route to the inner city of Babylon (there were seven lesser gates). It was dedicated to Ishtar, revered goddess of fertility, love, war and sex. Some scholars believe that, just as the Babylonian military and intellectual influence spread across the world, so too did their religion. There is speculation that the different names, Eostra or Ostara (a Germanic pagan goddess) and Easter, may originate from Ishtar. The Benedictine monk Saint Bede chronicled that Easter took its name from "Eostre", an Anglo Saxon goddess of spring. The Romans, in attempts at unity, were known to have combined festivals, their names and practices, in order to appease differing religious and pagan beliefs. If Easter is derived from Ishtar, that might make many of us think about the pagan origins of a major Christian festival.

Image: Model of the main procession street (Aj-ibur-shapu) towards Ishtar Gate by Gryffindor (Own work) [Public domain], via Wikimedia Commons

The Ishtar Gate and Processional Way (an artists' impression is shown above) were excavated by Robert Koldewey between 1899 and 1914. Its reconstruction in the Pergamon Museum in Berlin was completed in 1930, though some parts are so huge they are held in store.

As we have seen in the last chapter, records show that Nebuchadnezzar was responsible for bringing the kingdom of Judah to an end, when he destroyed Jerusalem in c 587 BC and took the Judeans into captivity.

Some records suggest that the captives would have entered the inner city through the Ishtar Gate but the accepted dates for these events make that unlikely.

However, there seems little doubt that the Ishtar Gate was completed during the time of the Jewish exile in Babylon.

There is a mass of information on the Internet about this, and a plethora of opinion, in which there is a considerable mixing of fact and fiction, myth, scientific study and archaeological findings. All this makes objective analysis very difficult. However, there are mythological references to the goddess Ishtar visiting hell and to the Ishtar Gate being the very entrance to hell. The depiction of 337 snake god images on the gate may have significance in Hebrew numerology, as the number 337 is said to represent hell.

You may feel that this connection and the Ishtar symbolism generally are overplayed. You may regard it all as just plain weird. Or you may come to the conclusion that this is an example of truth being stranger than fiction. Whatever your view, there is strong evidence to support the contention that the EU Parliament building is modelled on the Tower of Babel. Furthermore, there is no doubt that the Pergamon Altar and the Ishtar Gate stand in Berlin.

Is the circumstantial evidence enough to persuade you that these artifacts are "Satan's Throne" and "the Gateway to Hell" respectively?

Part 3: FULFILLED BIBLICAL PROPHECY

Chapter 11: GOD IS IN CONTROL

The most traumatic moment in Israel's history, prior to the birth of Jesus, was without doubt the sacking of Jerusalem by the Babylonians and the deportation of the Jewish remnant (about 50,000 people) in 587-6 BC. This event, more than any other in Israel's Old Testament history, caused national heartbreak. Not only were the Jewish people taken from the Promised Land and deported to Babylon. They were also separated from God's House, the Temple—the place where God's glory dwelt on the earth.

Taken to Babylon (modern Iraq), the Jewish exiles wept with regret for having grieved the Lord so deeply that he had withdrawn His protective blessing from the Land and over Jerusalem. This allowed the invading Babylonians to lay waste to everything, including the Temple that Solomon had built, with all its priceless furniture and artefacts. It is hard to even begin to imagine what it must have been like for these Jewish deportees, languishing in a pagan land, homesick for Zion, the City of God.

It was in this dire predicament that some of the Old Testament's greatest prophets were raised up to speak the Word of the Lord to the exiles, bringing sharp clarity about the sins that had brought them to this great distress, and words of profound comfort about the hope of restoration that God wanted to bring about in their lives.

It was into this vale of tears that Ezekiel, Daniel, Jeremiah, Isaiah and Habakkuk walked, bringing words that stirred up repentance for the past and mercy for the future.

These prophets knew the heart of God, which was to heal His people. But they also knew the mind of God, which was to show His people that one day they would be going home.

It was all in His plan.

When the time was right, God would reveal His sovereignty and move in the nations to make a way for His children, where it seemed there was no way—a way back to Jerusalem, the City of Peace, and to His ruined house, to rebuild it under the leadership of Zerubbabel and Joshua.

Prophecies Fulfilled

Let's remind ourselves that Biblical prophecy can basically be described as either *forthtelling* or foretelling. It either comes in the form of a prophet telling forth how God sees His people, particularly in terms of their recent past behaviour and their present circumstances. But it can also come in the form of foretelling—in the form of predictions about what will happen to God's children in the future.

When we look at what the prophets of the Exile were saying, we can see that they spoke a mixture of both. What is particularly impressive is the way they foresee and foretell everything that the Jewish people experience before, during and after the Exile. Tuned into the frequency of heaven, they discern exactly what God's plan is for His people. In dire distress, the people hear these words and hope arises in their hearts.

So, for example, Jeremiah prophesies about the destruction of Judah and Jerusalem by the invading Babylonians:

> *"I will summon all the peoples of the north and my servant Nebuchadnezzar king of Babylon," declares the LORD, and I will bring them against this land and its inhabitants and against all the surrounding nations. I will completely destroy them and make them an object of horror and scorn, and an everlasting ruin. I will banish from them the sounds of joy and gladness, the voices*

of bride and bridegroom, the sound of millstones and the light of the lamp. This whole country will become a desolate wasteland, and these nations will serve the king of Babylon seventy years. "But when the seventy years are fulfilled, I will punish the king of Babylon and his nation, the land of the Babylonians for their guilt," declares the LORD, and will make it desolate forever."

(Jeremiah 25:9-12, c 605 BC).

Here Jeremiah predicts not only the event of the Exile but its extent as well. He says that it will last 70 years, until the time that God punishes the Babylonians by destroying their empire.

The prophet Habakkuk also foresaw the Exile. Before it actually happened, Habakkuk complains bitterly that the wicked men and women of his own nation are prospering in Judah and asks God why they are being allowed to get away with their sinfulness. God replies that He is going to use the Babylonians to punish Judah.

Habakkuk is shocked and horrified; having the pagan Babylonian hordes overrun the nation is far worse than putting up with Judean wickedness! God answers this second complaint by saying that the Babylonians will be punished as well, in due course.

It is at this point that God speaks some beautiful and profound words to his prophet:

"Write down the revelation and make it plain on tablets so that a herald may run with it.

For the revelation awaits an appointed time; it speaks of the end

and will not prove false.

Though it linger, wait for it; it will certainly come and will not delay.

(Habakkuk 2:1-3)

Notice how God describes prophecy as "revelation" here. Revelation means "unveiling". The role of the prophet is to be a seer—to see what others cannot see, to seek out the revelation that God wants to share with them. Once that is received it is to be written down. Then it is to be communicated; it is to be heralded at the moment that God decrees. Every prophetic revelation that comes in the form of foretelling relates to a specific or appointed time (appointed by God that is). The prophet declares what is to come and then waits for the moment when what is predicted actually occurs. It may sometimes linger, but the prophet and indeed the people are to wait and believe, knowing that if God has spoken He is never early or late, but right on time.

The Book of Habakkuk shows that God is in control and hears our prayers, but His answers may not be what we expect! He has a plan and it will be carried through to completion by whomsoever He chooses. Furthermore, the book also shows that sin will be punished.

God's Surprising Servant

The words of the prophets sometimes contained dramatic surprises. Perhaps the best example in this timeframe is the revelation that God was going to use a pagan King to secure the return of the Jewish remnant to Jerusalem. That man's name is Cyrus, King of the Persian Empire—the Empire that replaced the Babylonians. Here is Isaiah:

> *"This is what the LORD says to his anointed, to Cyrus, whose right hand I take hold of to subdue nations before him and to strip kings of their armour, to open doors before him so that gates will not be shut: I will go before you and will level the mountains; I will break down gates of bronze and cut through bars of iron. I will give you hidden treasures, riches stored in secret places, so that you may know that I am the LORD, the God of Israel, who summons you by name. For the sake of Jacob my servant, of Israel my chosen, I summon you by name and bestow on you a title of honour, though you do not acknowledge me. I am the LORD, and there is no other; apart from me there is no God. I will strengthen you, though you have not acknowledged me, so that from the*

rising of the sun to the place of its setting people may know there is none besides me. I am the LORD, and there is no other.

(Isaiah 45:1-6 c 688 BC)

I am the Lord ... who says of Cyrus, 'He is my shepherd and will accomplish all that I please; he will say of Jerusalem, "Let it be rebuilt," and of the temple, "Let its foundations be laid."'

(Isaiah 44:28)

God named Cyrus, before he was born, as the person who would guarantee the return of a Jewish remnant to Jerusalem. Jeremiah 25:9-12 (see above) and Jeremiah 29:10 both confirm that God would bring the Judeans back to their homeland whilst Daniel 5:17-30 shows that the Babylonian (Chaldean) Empire would be given to the Medes and Persians. On the night of the latter prophecy, Babylon was conquered and the king, Belshazzar, was killed.

Truly God is in control!

The Seventy Years

As mentioned in Chapter 10, there is much debate amongst scholars about how the time of the people of Judah in Babylon can be squared with the 70 year period mentioned in Scripture.

In trying to resolve this anomaly it is important to admit that it's much easier to determine when the Exile technically ended than when it began. We know it came to an end in 538BC when King Cyrus decided that the peoples and tribes that had been forced into Exile by his enemies, the Babylonians, should be allowed to return to their own lands and to worship their own God or gods. Clearly Cyrus was something of a man of mercy. He was appalled by the displacement of nations by the Babylonians. He was also arguably the first religious pluralist in history—a man who respected other peoples' rights to worship in a way that was true to their ethnic traditions. So it was that Cyrus said to the leaders of the Jewish exiles, Zerubabbel and Joshua, "You can go back to Judah and to Jerusalem, and you can have whatever Temple artefacts we can still find returned to you." This all happened in 538BC, when 50,000 Jews started the long journey back to Jerusalem to begin work rebuilding the Temple.

When, then, did the Exile technically begin? It should be noted that the people of Judah were taken into captivity in three stages: 605 BC (see Daniel 1:1-6), 597 BC (see 2 Chronicles 36:5-10 and 2 Kings 24:15-17), and 587-586 BC (see 2 Kings 25). If we take this first of these (the furthest in time from 538BC) the maximum time is not 70 but 67 years (605-538 BC).

How are we to resolve this?

Looking at the references in Jeremiah 25 and 29 in more detail may help our understanding.

Jeremiah 25:9-12 says:

"I will summon all the peoples of the north and my servant Nebuchadnezzar king of Babylon," declares the LORD, "and I will bring them against this land and its inhabitants and against all the surrounding nations. I will completely destroy them and make them an object of horror and scorn, and an everlasting ruin. I will banish from them the sounds of joy and gladness, the voices of bride and bridegroom, the sound of millstones and the light of the lamp. This whole country will become a desolate wasteland, and these nations will serve the king of Babylon seventy years. "But when the seventy years are fulfilled, I will punish the king of Babylon and his nation, the land of the Babylonians for their guilt," declares the LORD,"

Then Jeremiah 29:10 says:

"This is what the LORD says: "When seventy years are completed for Babylon, I will come to you and fulfil my good promise to bring you back to this place."

The text clearly indicates that "nations will serve the king of Babylon seventy years" and that the 70 years is "for Babylon".

There is therefore good reason to suggest that the period of 70 years relates to the time of Chaldean ascendancy, beginning with

Nabopolasser's capture of Nineveh and Harran in 609 BC (where he defeated the Assyrian Empire and established the Babylonian Empire), through Nebuchadnezzar's reign to his son Belshazzar's downfall in 539 BC (establishing the Persian Empire). This is a period of 70 years!

2 Chronicles 36:20-23 is also helpful, although please note that 2 Chronicles is a work of history rather than prophecy, and therefore looks back at what has happened, rather than forward to what hasn't:

"He carried into exile to Babylon the remnant, who escaped from the sword, and they became servants to him and his successors until the kingdom of Persia came to power. The land enjoyed its Sabbath rests; all the time of its desolation it rested, until the seventy years were completed in fulfilment of the word of the LORD spoken by Jeremiah.

In the first year of Cyrus king of Persia, in order to fulfil the word of the LORD spoken by Jeremiah, the LORD moved the heart of Cyrus king of Persia to make a proclamation throughout his realm and also to put it in writing:"

Again, close reading shows that the 70 years in this Scripture can be interpreted as relating to the period of the rule of the Babylonian Empire. On that basis, the 48 year desolation of Jerusalem, 586-538 BC, does not undermine the 70 years of 2 Chronicles and Jeremiah.

Lastly, the 70 year prophecy of Jeremiah is referred to in the book of Daniel:

"In the first year of Darius son of Xerxes (a Mede by descent), who was made ruler over the Babylonian kingdom—in the first year of his reign, I, Daniel, understood from the Scriptures, according to the word of the Lord given to Jeremiah the prophet, that the desolation of Jerusalem would last seventy years. So I turned to the Lord God and pleaded with him in prayer and petition, in fasting, and in sackcloth and ashes."

(Daniel 9:1-3).

In this passage it also seems at first glance that Daniel believes Jerusalem would lay desolate for 70 years—but if this is the case, why is he so earnest in his prayer to God on behalf of his people?

This segment comes in the first year of the rule of the Medes and Persians—i.e. 539/538 B.C. At this point, Jerusalem has lain desolate for only 48 years, so surely there would be another 22 years to go?

Daniel seems keen on the idea that the seventy years is in fact now over and that the exiled people of Judah should return to Jerusalem as God had promised. This can only be the case if Daniel understood the seventy years as referring to the length of time that Babylon would rule, and not to the desolation of Jerusalem. So, like the writer of Chronicles, Daniel understood that after Jerusalem was destroyed it would be desolate for the remainder of the seventy-year period. Hence Daniel says that "the desolation of Jerusalem would last [the] seventy years." Now that the seventy years of Babylonian ascendancy is up, Daniel is asking God "How much longer?" As it turns out, he had less than a year to wait until Cyrus II gave the decree allowing the people of Judah to return to Jerusalem.

God Rules over All

A church once held a prayer meeting in response to critical and desperate events on the world stage. It seemed like things were going from bad to worse and that the nations were poised to descend into great darkness. As the people of God began to pray, many of the prayers focused on situations on the ground, admitting that things looked hopeless, but asking God to intervene. This focus on the ground level problems continued until one man, not known for academic brilliance or for rhetorical eloquence, stood to his feet and started to thank God.

"I thank you Jesus, that even though the world is in a mess, you're still on the throne in heaven."

With that the whole tone of the meeting changed. Instead of focusing on the problems, and praying with forlorn hearts, people began to focus on the Lord, worshipping him for being sovereign over all the earth and in control of the whole world and its events.

People began to sing "Our God reigns."

People began to confess that nothing ever takes God by surprise.

People began to do what the prophets of old used to do—remind others how big God is, not how big the problems were.

When you look back at what God's chosen people went through, while they were in Babylon, it's hard to imagine that they were full of faith and hope. But when the prophets started to prophesy, they realised that even though they were in a mess, God was still on His throne. They reminded themselves that God rules over all the nations—not just the Jewish people, but over men like King Cyrus and over the Persians as well as the Babylonians. He even has dates and times in which people who do not even know Him will obey His will! That is astonishing and comforting in equal measure.

It is worth remembering, as we approach the subject of the End Times, that every prophecy about these days "awaits its appointed time." God is in control and He alone knows the date and the hour when His Son will return.

Our task, as His children, is to look at what is happening in the world and indeed in the church and, however desperate, to remember that these are signs that were prophesied two thousand or more years ago and that there is nothing occurring in the world today that is outside God's plan.

So thank God for the miracle of fulfilled prophecy.

And instead of looking down, look up and say: "I thank you Jesus, that even though the world is in a mess, you're still on the throne in heaven."

This will be particularly important in the next few chapters as we consider for a moment the devil's plans.

Even though these are wicked and destructive, never forget that He who is in you (Jesus) is greater than he who is at work in the world (the devil).

Chapter 12: KNOW YOUR ENEMY

The Bible is the story of God's chosen people, the first coming of Jesus, His ministry on Earth, His death and resurrection, the founding of Christianity and the grafting in of the Gentiles. It also foretells how the story will end. Israel (the Jewish people) will suffer all sorts of trials and tribulations because of their disobedience and because Satan was, and continues to be, opposed to their existence. The same is true for the church.

Who is Satan and why is he opposed to mankind in general and Israel and the church in particular?

Answering these questions requires some speculation. The hypothesis that follows does not have full Scriptural authority and should be treated with caution. Scripture references are only given where the Bible passage clearly supports the case being made.

In Hebrew the word satan means adversary. Satan came to be used as the name for a fallen angel who rebelled against God and sought to take God's throne for himself. The Bible gives little information about Satan's origins and downfall. In Isaiah and Ezekiel there are references to the fall of the "morning star", translated as Lucifer, which some interpret as relating to Satan, while others suggest it relates to the King of Babylon.

There have been many hypotheses over the centuries: some suggest Satan was a very (or perhaps the most) senior angel and his pride and selfishness led him to rebel against God's decision to create man. As far as I am aware there is no Scriptural foundation for this theory.

Another proposition is that God so loves mankind that He has given us freedom of choice. In order to have freedom of choice there has to be an option. God gives us everything we need in order to make an informed choice about the Gospel (the Good News) and the reality of Jesus as our Messiah. The Good News about Jesus will continue to be preached for as long as God ordains, and during that time Satan is permitted to roam the Earth. Again, though some aspects can be inferred, there is no clear Scriptural basis to confirm this view.

The Adversary's Plan

Perhaps Satan's most significant advantage is that many people do not believe he exists! His depiction as some sort of demonic cartoon character has encouraged the view that the devil is a mythical oddity of no significance to 21st century man. However, we can see from Scripture that Jesus took him very seriously and even though Satan's destruction is assured, in the meantime he and his demons strive to undermine God's plan.

So what can we legitimately infer from Scripture about Satan's plan? The Apostle Paul once wrote that we are not to be ignorant of Satan's schemes. So what is he scheming?

Satan knows what the Bible says and that the Book of Revelation shows that Jesus will return to Jerusalem to take His rightful place on the throne of David, as King of the Jews. He will rule His people and the world from Jerusalem. Satan's options for preventing this (and preventing his ultimate banishment to "the lake of burning sulphur" Revelation 20:10) were and are:

1) to tempt Jesus to sin and so become unworthy as Saviour
2) to destroy Jesus;
3) to disperse the Jews and fragment and undermine their national identity, and/or

4) to annihilate all Jews so that Jesus has no Jewish Kingdom to which to return and rule;
5) to prevent the establishment of a Jewish nation state (Israel); and/or
6) to destroy Israel or Jerusalem, or to divide Jerusalem (i.e. ensure control remains in the hands of non-believers).

He tried the first and was resisted. He tried the second and was spectacularly defeated when Jesus rose from the dead. The third, fourth, fifth and sixth have been ongoing through history. Again, I emphasise the huge significance of the reestablishment of Israel as a nation state in 1948 and the reunification of Jerusalem in 1967. The Temple Mount, however, remains in the hands of Gentiles. It is to this we must turn now.

The Temple Mount

The Temple Mount warrants closer examination. The Jews, or more accurately those practicing Judaism, consider the Temple Mount to be the place where God chose to manifest His divine presence (Isaiah 8:18; Psalm 9:11). Having said that, there has been much confusion about whether the Temple Mount is on Mount Zion.

From 2 Samuel 5:6-9 it is clear that Mount Zion was a fortress that King David captured from the Jebusites. He renamed it the City of David and developed and expanded the site. The scope of the City of David can be seen from modern day archaeological excavations. Solomon, King David's son and successor, built the first Temple on Mount Moriah in 957 BC (2 Chronicles 3:1-2). Mount Moriah is probably synonymous with what we now call the Temple Mount, though its exact location has not been confirmed. It seems that with the building of the Temple the term "Zion" was expanded to include the Mount and subsequently the whole of Jerusalem and the people of Israel (hence "Zionism"). This collective term can be seen in Isaiah 40:9, Jeremiah 31:12 and Zechariah 9:13. The first

Temple was destroyed by the Babylonians in 586 BC.

Zion became a term used for the people of God (Isaiah 60:14) and this continues into the New Testament era (Hebrews 12:22; Revelation 4:1). Peter refers to Jesus as the Cornerstone of Zion (1 Peter 2:4-6).

The second Temple was built under the direction of Zerubbabel in 516 BC and destroyed by the Romans in 70 AD. Jewish tradition maintains that there will be a third Temple on the Temple Mount and that its design has been prophesied in Ezekiel 40-47.

Sunni Muslims consider the Mount to be the "Noble Sanctuary", the third most holy site in Islam. It is revered as the location to which Mohammad was transported for his ascent to heaven. The Dome of the Rock and the al-Aqsa Mosque were built on the Mount after the Muslim conquest of Jerusalem in 637 AD. The Dome of the Rock, completed in 692 AD, is in the middle of the Temple Mount, on the site where many (but not all) Biblical scholars believe that the Third Temple should be built.

The question remains, why is the Temple Mount still under Muslim control? In 1967 the Jordanians, with the help of Syria and Egypt, attacked Israel. Prior to the 1967 "Six-Day War" Jordan controlled East Jerusalem, including the Temple Mount, and the West Bank. Israel's armed forces defeated the attack and occupied East Jerusalem and the West Bank. In the aftermath of the war Israel agreed to the return of the control of the Temple Mount to the Islamic Waqf (guardians of Muslim holy sites). This gesture has not led to peace and reconciliation. The Temple Mount is an enclave within Israeli controlled Jerusalem. Muslims have been granted authority to manage the Temple Mount in accordance with their traditions, while Israel continues to have technical control of the site and monitors access. To add to the confusion, the Palestinian Authority claims sovereignty over the Temple Mount.

So to summarise: Zion was the fortress that King David captured from the Jebusites. He renamed it the City of David. It is thought that the location of Zion expanded to include the Temple Mount, and subsequently Jerusalem and the people of Israel. Following the destruction of Jerusalem the name Mount Zion referred to its present location across the valley to the south of the walled city. While the physical location of Zion may have changed over the years, the spiritual relevance has remained constant.

A Concrete Sign

I hope this provides some understanding of why the Temple Mount is almost certainly the most contested religious site in the world. There can be little doubt that Jerusalem has something utterly unique about it. Considering its size and location, it is truly amazing how significant it has been and continues to be in world affairs. But then it is the focal point of End Times prophecy so why should we be at all surprised by this? I believe we should keep a very close watch on all news and information relating to events in Jerusalem.

Of particular interest are the ongoing rumours about the building of a third Temple on the Temple Mount. Many Christians believe that if the End Times prophecies are to come true in any literal sense, then a third Temple will have to have been constructed before history reaches its climax.

This would indeed be a "concrete sign."

In the next chapter we will look at another sign of the End Times, the sign of Noah.

Noah has been making something of a comeback in contemporary culture.

Sir Ridley Scott has recently released a blockbuster movie, with Russell Crowe starring as Noah.

Is it just mere coincidence that Noah is centre stage in people's imaginations right now?

Or is it a sign of the times?

Chapter 13: IN THE DAYS OF NOAH

As it was in the days of Noah, so it will be at the coming of the Son of Man.

Matthew 24:36-37

Jesus likens the characteristics of End Times world activities and conditions to the circumstances prevalent in the days of Noah. This parallel is repeated in Luke 17:26. In Luke 17:28 the comparison is expanded to include the conditions in Sodom during the time leading up to Lot's departure from that city. Jesus warns that the End Times will be characterised by an extreme immorality whose closest parallels in history are the conditions before the destruction of the world in the time of Noah (the Flood) and those that prevailed in Sodom and Gomorrah in the time of Abraham.

So what exactly were these conditions like?

The account of Noah's exceptional righteousness and the exceptional amorality of his culture are given in Genesis 6. What seems clear from the opening of Genesis 6 is that Satan had been very busy trying to pollute and pervert the human race. This had come in the form of a very demonic and deviant form of intercourse between "the sons of God" and "the daughters of men" (Genesis 6: 1-4). Most scholars agree that the phrase "sons of God" refers to fallen angels, while "the daughters of men" refers to human women. These fallen angels had sexual relations with human women and in doing so crossed every known boundary. Furthermore, the offspring of these illicit unions was a race called "the Nephilim"—

gigantic beings that roamed the earth. Some think that the gods and heroes of Greek and Roman mythology may in fact be these Nephilim.

From all of this we can see why the writer of Genesis 6 says that the earth was full of wickedness and evil thoughts (v 5), violence (v 11) and sexual corruption (v 12). Materialism, violence, corruption and immorality were accepted as the norm. The same sorts of conditions were witnessed later on in Sodom and Gomorrah. Genesis 19:1-9 says there was widespread, blatant, violent and predatory homosexual behaviour there.

All this is bad news. But the good news is that Noah had a prophetic sensibility and that his intimate relationship with God enabled him to hear divine warnings about what was to come. While the rest of the people seemed hell-bent on living a godless and immoral life, Noah "walked with God" and "found favour in the eyes of the Lord". He was obedient to God and, as head of his family, took full responsibility for his household. Hearing God's voice he built an ark and then navigated his family to safety.

Noah and his family escaped the Flood that God sent to cleanse the earth.

Noah's World and Ours

What has this all to do with the End Times? The answer is everything. Jesus warned that society would start to resemble Noah's world as the climax of history approached. He added that cities would resemble Sodom. In this He was not alone in the New Testament.

Paul describes the conditions of the End Times in 2 Timothy 3:1-9:

> *"But mark this: There will be terrible times in the last days. People will be lovers of themselves, lovers of money, boastful, proud, abusive, disobedient to their parents, ungrateful, unholy, without love, unforgiving, slanderous, without self-control, brutal, not*

lovers of the good treacherous, rash, conceited, lovers of pleasure rather than lovers of God—having a form of godliness but denying its power. Have nothing to do with such people. They are the kind who worm their way into homes and gain control over gullible women, who are loaded down with sins and are swayed by all kinds of evil desires, always learning but never able to come to a knowledge of the truth. Just as Jannes and Jambres opposed Moses, so also these teachers oppose the truth.They are men of depraved minds, who, as far as the faith is concerned, are rejected. But they will not get very far because, as in the case of those men, their folly will be clear to everyone."

This description could have come right out of Noah's diary! And, more disturbingly still, it could come from ours as well. The conditions of the world today are very similar to those that Paul describes and Noah witnessed.

The Age of Tolerance

At the same time, this is where Bible truth is set for a collision course with something that has taken a strong hold of almost everybody's minds in contemporary culture. I am referring of course to political correctness.

I don't doubt that some readers will have been, and some will continue to be, challenged by what the Bible has to say about moral standards and behaviour. Instinctively, I want to soften the words. I have been brought up to find the middle ground, seek consensus, soothe and placate, and to do my utmost to avoid confrontation.

In recent years I have felt an increasing unease as a seemingly very reasonable form of humanitarian liberalism has spread and diluted what I consider to be fundamental moral values. Fear of offending encourages us to water down any view that appears contrary to perceived political correctness. We are subtly encouraged to compromise in the cause of peaceful coexistence in a pluralistic society and invariably finding the middle ground sounds both reasonable and sensible. Luke-warmness is accordingly the order of the day and, with clever packaging and gentle coaxing, immorality is made to look as if it is enlightened tolerance. The State condones what is clearly described as unwholesome behaviour in the Bible and calls it "an alternative lifestyle" or "preferred orientation", condemning anyone who suggests that it might actually be unwholesome. Unborn babies are killed in the name of freedom of choice and convenience. Genetic engineering is encouraged in the furtherance of scientific research.

We dumb down our Christian heritage in the name of broad-minded pragmatism and multiculturalism. We use elegant language to conceal our move away from what I believe are fundamental truths that have been given to us for a purpose. We exploit the poor and call it the luck of the draw or self-preservation. We encourage idleness in the name of welfare, while managing to ignore the real needs of those who cannot cope with our bureaucratic systems. We let children have free rein and call it free expression (leaving them unprepared for the real world).

I am convinced that this suppression of the values we once held dear is undermining our spiritual wellbeing. As a nation we worship other gods—the god of self, rights, money, materialism, humanism, sex, greed, exploitation. We allow power to be abused and accept it as political astuteness, the way of the world, or not our problem. We pollute the air with profanity, pornography, and the portrayal of extreme violence; all in the name of freedom of speech. We contaminate the environment with chemicals and pestilence, fumes and waste, in pursuit of short-term gain. We see the banks—once bastions of our economic wellbeing—managed by gamblers who use our collective high street deposits for speculative trading, without any interest in the people or the products of the companies and ventures in which they "invest". We ridicule the values of the past in the name of enlightenment. If we object to this move away from Christian principles we are accused of fundamentalism, or prejudice, or fanaticism, or narrow-mindedness, or bigotry, or discrimination.

So if you ask me whether the conditions of the world today look like those that Noah saw, then I'd say yes, without reservation.

It all reminds me of frogs. I have been told that if a frog is placed in a pan of boiling water, it will jump out. However, if it is placed in a pan of cold water, and the temperature of the water is slowly increased, the frog will not notice until it is too late.

Political correctness has been, and continues to be, taken to ridiculous and ungodly extremes. Legislation, ostensibly designed to protect human rights and encourage civil liberties, is hijacked by vociferous minorities demanding equality, acceptance, endorsement and even, in some cases, the requirement that their views or "lifestyle preferences" should be taught in schools. It is much easier to take a "live and let live", "turn a blind eye" or "who cares" attitude, than it is to object to this creeping "liberalisation". Standing against this drift has already proved challenging for some: it is not difficult to visualise circumstances where opposing ungodliness in our society today could be as hazardous as protesting and prophesying against the trend usually was for the Old Testament prophets!

Truly, like Noah, we need to walk closely with God in a generation such as ours.

It's Getting Wider and Worse

Are we different from earlier generations, any of which may have considered their society venal and corrupt? I suggest that it is not the nature but the scale and proliferation of immorality that has reached unprecedented levels right now. It is the pervasion of perversion that is so staggering today. Yes, previous generations have witnessed times of great social wickedness and corruption, great outbreaks of immorality in which every line has been crossed, as in Noah's time. But ours is an exceptional age of darkness. There never has been a time like ours where the extent and the increase in wickedness is before our eyes all of the time. Never has it been tougher to be like Noah—a person of righteousness.

Since the advent of television in about 1950, and the

development of mobile phone technology from the 1980s, there has been an explosion of instantly available immorality of all kinds in picture and video formats, from "soft" to "hard core". These place before peoples' eyes images of all kinds of violent, barbaric and brutal behaviour, persuading them over time that this gross abnormality is the "new normal". Combined with the availability of immediate "lines of credit", which has encouraged and facilitated the possibility of near instant gratification of virtually any desire, people have embraced a hedonism that denies the need for, and existence of, God.

I don't want to belabour the point but I am convinced that there has been a staggering increase of all the Noah-based behavioural comparators that can be identified.

We really are "in the days of Noah".

Part 4: END TIMES PROPHECY

Chapter 14: THE BIBLICAL TIMELINE

Supposing the Bible does provide a timeline to the Second Coming of Jesus, how far are we along that line?

So far we have studied a wide selection of fulfilled prophecies, and a variety of signs and unusual events that may have spiritual significance. Now I want to focus on what might be termed, or certainly used as, a centre line for examining End Times prophetic scriptures. I am going to do this by giving a narrative summary of Matthew 24, as a base line for building a framework of Biblical prophecy relating to things that have been fulfilled, are being fulfilled and will be fulfilled. The account will follow the chronology of Matthew24 but I will also refer to the Gospel of Mark, which covers many of these events, albeit in a different style.

Two Questions at Once

At the start of Matthew 24 the disciples make a remark to Jesus about the beauty and splendour of the Temple buildings—the setting for their discussion. They are shocked by His response. Jesus tells them that the Temple will be utterly destroyed, not one stone left on another. This startling prophetic statement leads them to ask two questions:

1. "When will this (i.e. the destruction of the Temple) happen?"
2. "What will be the sign of your coming and of the end of the age?"

It's important to understand before going any further that these would not have been separate in the minds of the disciples. The disciples were Jewish followers of Jesus and to a Jewish way of thinking the destruction of the Temple would be the end of the world. In their hearts, the end of the Temple and the end of the world amount to the same thing.

In Jesus' mind, however, these are two separate issues. Yes, the destruction of the Temple might seem like the end of the world to the Jewish people but in reality the events surrounding the Temple's destruction—which would happen forty years later in AD 70—would not constitute the climax of history, or the time of His return.

In Jesus' mind, the destruction of the Temple at the hands of the Romans in AD 70 can be linked to the climax of history only in this regard—that the tragic and appalling events surrounding the sacking of Jerusalem and the obliteration of the Temple would be a kind of dress rehearsal for the even more woeful events surrounding the End Times.

AD 70 is the trailer for the main feature, when God calls an end to human history and sends His Son to return to planet earth.

Answers to Question One

So what does Jesus say in answer to the two questions? Before He answers them directly, He warns the disciples against being deceived by people falsely claiming to be Christ (the Greek word for the Hebrew "Messiah", meaning "The Anointed One"). This admonition against deception by false prophets and Messiahs is a theme that continues throughout Matthew 24.

Jesus then begins by answering the first question, about the destruction of Jerusalem. This is most clearly given in Mark 13:20-24:

> *"When you see Jerusalem being surrounded by armies, you will know that its desolation is near. Then let those who are in Judea flee to the mountains, let those in the city get out, and let those in*

the country not enter the city. For this is the time of punishment in fulfilment of all that has been written. How dreadful it will be in those days for pregnant women and nursing mothers! There will be great distress in the land and wrath against this people. They will fall by the sword and will be taken as prisoners to all the nations. Jerusalem will be trampled on by the Gentiles until the times of the Gentiles are fulfilled."

As I've already indicated, the exact fulfilment of this prophecy came forty years later in AD 70. It is interesting to note that the Roman General Vespasian was in the process of establishing a siege around Jerusalem when he was recalled to Rome to be installed as Emperor. Thus a lull occurred which allowed many besieged victims to escape the city before Vespasian's son, General Titus, continued and completed the assault which was to lead to the destruction of the city and the Temple.

Please note as well that there was nothing metaphorical about the siege of Jerusalem and its destruction and that those who knew what Jesus had said, and were obedient to His advice, escaped. From that day to this, the most sacred place for the Jews has been "trampled on by the Gentiles," in direct fulfilment of Biblical prophecy.

Answers to Question Two

In answering the second question, which has two overlapping parts (the sign of Christ's coming and the end of the age), Jesus addresses the second part first: that is to say, the sign of the end of the age. He summarises several signs before giving the sign. He makes it clear that while various catastrophic events constitute the "birth-pains" for what is to come—and these along with persecution will cause many people to turn away from the faith—they are not the final sign. The sign is given in v 14: *"And this gospel of the kingdom will be preached in the whole world as a testimony to all nations, and then the end will come."*

The proclamation of the Good News about the Kingdom

of God can be seen as the required culmination of the "Great Commission"—the task given to the disciples in Matthew 28, to go and make disciples of all nations. God wants to make sure that everyone on the earth has an opportunity to hear and respond to the Good News before the end comes.

In these early verses of Matthew 24 Jesus emphasises the need for His followers to stand firm during the labour pains that indicate the imminence of the "birth" of the final inauguration of the Kingdom of God on earth, which will be achieved when Jesus returns.

The Abomination of Desolation

From verse 15 to 25 of Matthew 24 the focus of Jesus' warnings narrows to Israel. He says that when "the abomination that causes desolation" is seen in the "holy place", it is time to flee. This climactic and terrible event will take place during a season of intense deception and great global distress. In spite of these cataclysmic occurrences, Jesus does not say that we should pray against these things happening, rather that they don't happen in winter, or on the Sabbath.

What is "the abomination that causes desolation"? It seems that the events of AD 70 were a "model" or "shadow" of what will happen at the end of the age. When Titus destroyed the Temple, he committed a sacrilegious and blasphemous act by setting up a pagan idol on the site. This once again is like a first century teaser for an End Times main feature. Prophecies relating to the End Times (notably 2 Thessalonians 2:4 and Revelation 13:14-15) say that the Antichrist will declare himself god, set up an image of himself in the Temple, and order everyone to worship it. This is the second and final "abomination" that mocks God.

Jesus goes on to say (Matthew 24:24) that some false Christs and false prophets will be so convincing that even the "elect" (well established, strong Christians) may be deceived, and that things will be so bad that no one would survive if the "days had not been cut short."

Christ's Return

Jesus then addresses part one of question two—what will be the sign of His coming?

Jesus return will be unmistakeable! If we think that the Messiah *might* have come, then He hasn't! If we don't believe that Christ can make His second and glorious coming to planet Earth obvious to everyone, then we seriously underestimate his power and, authority.

In the closing verses of Matthew 24, Jesus urges us to be both watchful and prepared; His return will be swift and sudden. We are not told the "day or the hour" (verse 36) and, as mentioned earlier, it seems clear that we should not speculate on these matters. However, we do have some indication of the events leading up to the end of the age, and that things will be as they were "in the days of Noah" (verse 37).

Chapter 15: SIGNS OF THE END TIMES

Have you ever noticed how the best teachers make hard things simple? Jesus was just like that. He brought the deepest truths of heaven to earth in plain, simple language that everyone could understand. No one in history has ever been able to match Him in this regard. His proverbs and parables not only made His revelation memorable; it also made it accessible to those who had ears to hear and eyes to see.

At the risk of doing the opposite of Jesus—by making simple things hard—I want to introduce you to an important technical term from Christian theology. It's the word "eschatology." The New Testament was originally written in a kind of market-place version of the Greek language. In this popular form of Greek the word *eschaton* means "last thing" (plural, *eschata*, "last things") while logos means speech.

What then is eschatology? It is the ability to speak in a coherent way about the last things. The last things refer to the final facts of history. Anyone who has studied Biblical eschatology will hopefully be able to talk meaningfully about what the Bible warns concerning the End Times.

As the old theological professor once said, as he introduced a lecture on this topic, "If you don't know what eschatology is, it isn't the end of the world!"

Made More Certain

But actually that might not be true. If we don't know what the

Bible teaches about the End Times it very likely will be the end of the world for us when the final facts predicted in Scripture begin. We must take care therefore not to be ignorant about eschatology. How can we be vigilant if we don't know what it is we are supposed to be watching out for?

In chapter 1 we looked at ten Scriptures about the restoration of Israel and the return of the Jewish people to their homeland that were miraculously fulfilled in 1948. I now want to examine a few sample Scriptures relating to End Times prophecies, with some thoughts on their significance. Where dates are shown, they are approximate. Some points from earlier chapters are repeated, for emphasis and easy reference.

Let's begin by reminding ourselves that Biblical prophecy is authoritative and accurate. Just as the Biblical prophecies about Christ's First Coming were fulfilled with astonishing precision, the ones about his Second Coming will be. As the apostle Peter said:

> *And we have the word of the prophets made more certain, and you will do well to pay attention to it, as to a light shining in a dark place, until the day dawns and the morning star rises in your hearts. Above all, you must understand that no prophecy of Scripture came about by the prophet's own interpretation of things. For prophecy never had its origin in the human will, but prophets, though human, spoke from God as they were carried along by the Holy Spirit.*
>
> 2 Peter 1:19-21 (written c 67 AD)

It stands to reason that because a great number of Biblical prophecies have been fulfilled about Christ's First Coming, and confirmed by witnesses and historical records, we can be "more certain" that the remainder will be fulfilled. Though written by human hands, Biblical prophecies were inspired by the Holy Spirit. This was one reason why Jesus was hard on his contemporaries for failing to see the connection between his ministry and the prophecies in the Hebrew Bible about Him. He castigated them by saying, "you did not recognise the time of God's coming to you" (Luke 19:44).

Jesus held the crowd, and in particular the Pharisees, accountable for not recognising the fulfilment of Scriptural prophecy. To those who have seen and believed that Jesus is the Light of the World, there is no need to be "in the dark" about his Second Coming in the way that so many religiously minded people were about his First. As the apostle Paul wrote: "But you, brothers, are not in darkness so that this day should surprise you like a thief" (1 Thessalonians 5:4, written c 50 AD). Non-believers are "in the dark" and will be surprised (something of an understatement!) when the Lord returns. The same is not the case for true believers. While it is true that we do not know the hour or the day of the Lord's return, we do have prophetically predicted signs of the End Times, which we can relate to unfolding world events.

In the pages that follow I will mention more of this "read across" quality between Scripture and current affairs.

Technological Advances

The prophet Daniel (writing during the time of the Exile in the 6th century BC) prophesied that there will come a time when the righteous and the wicked will be resurrected. As that time approaches the ability to travel all over the world will be radically transformed and human knowledge increase:

> *Multitudes who sleep in the dust of the earth will awake, some to everlasting life and others to shame and everlasting contempt. Those who are wise will shine like the brightness of the heavens and those who lead many to righteousness will shine like the stars forever and ever. As for you Daniel, conceal these words and seal up the book until the end of time. Many will run to and fro and knowledge will increase.*
>
> (Daniel 12:2-4)

Until the 20th century most people did not travel very far from home during their lives. Some historians suggest that the vast majority stayed within twenty miles of their birthplace. Today we can fly virtually anywhere in the world in less than twenty-four hours.

Furthermore, until recently, knowledge and technology were relatively constant. However, in the last fifty years there has been a phenomenal increase in technological innovation and the capability and capacity to acquire, store and access knowledge.

In the twentieth century, the progress of science was so vast and fast that many people claimed that mankind had reached its full potential. However, the use of this same scientific knowledge to destroy six million Jews and, using the atomic bomb, hundreds of thousands of Japanese citizens must call into question what that "full potential" might signify! Mankind may have advanced scientifically, but this knowledge has not only given people the ability to save lives (through, for example, medical research and treatment) but also to destroy nations. Without doubt this is something that the Biblical prophets foresaw, as exemplified by the apostle John in the last book of the Bible, Revelation:

The nations were angry and your wrath has come. The time has come for judging the dead and for rewarding your servants, the prophets, your saints and those who reverence your name, both small and great and for destroying those who destroy the earth.

Revelation 11:18 (written 95 AD).

Notice the phrase, "those who destroy the earth." Human beings now have the capacity to destroy planet Earth. We have the technology to cause untold ecological havoc, as prophesied once again by the apostle John in his final years:

The sixth angel poured out his bowl on the great river, the Euphrates, and its water was dried up so that the way would be prepared for the kings from the east.

Revelation 16:12

It's revealing and indeed sobering to note that in 1993 Turkey finished construction on the Ataturk Dam, which can stop the flow of the Euphrates River, just as the apostle John predicted.

Here's another of his predictions:

For three and a half days, people from every tribe, language and nation will gaze at their bodies and refuse them burial. The inhabitants of the earth will gloat over them and will celebrate by sending each other gifts because these two prophets had tormented those who live on the earth.

Revelation 11:9

Here once again we can see how Biblical prophecy foretells the technological advances of our own times. How would it be possible for people from every nation in the world to view events in one location on the earth over a three-and-a-half day period? Only in the last few decades, with the advent of TV and associated satellite communications, could this prophecy be fulfilled. Only in very recent times has it become possible for the entire population of the globe to "gloat" over the corpses of those caught up in the slaughter of the End Times.

The Siege of Jerusalem

This is the Word of the Lord concerning Israel. The Lord, who stretches out the heavens, who lays the foundation of the earth and who forms the spirit of man within him declares: "I am going to make Jerusalem a cup that sends all the surrounding peoples reeling. Judah will be besieged as well as Jerusalem. On that day, when all the nations of the earth are gathered against her, I will make Jerusalem an immovable rock for all the nations. All who try to move it will be severely injured."

Zechariah 12:1-3 (written c 530 BC)

God says Jerusalem will be the focal point at the end of the age. All nations on the earth will descend on the holy city. God also makes it clear that nations that attack Jerusalem will not succeed.

It is interesting to note that much of the unrest in the Middle East today relates to the existence of Israel and the control of Jerusalem. As we have discussed, after a worldwide exile, Israel re-established its nationhood on 14 May 1948 and Jerusalem was re-unified after the 6 Day War in 1967.

When will this unsuccessful End Times attack on Jerusalem take place? Let's listen to what the prophet Ezekiel predicted:

> *I will go up against the land of unwalled villages. I will go against those who are at rest and live securely, all of them living without walls and having no bars or gates.*
>
> Ezekiel 38:11 (written c 580 BC)

It seems that in the run-up to the End Times siege of Jerusalem by all the nations of the world (as opposed to just one nation in AD 70, namely the Romans), Israel will lower its guard in a time of seeming security, peace and prosperity.

The Biblical prophets tell us what's going to happen to the armies of the earth as they seek to destroy Jerusalem and the Jewish people. Their end is described in graphic terms—in language that evokes pictures of what happened to the victims of the atomic bomb:

> *This will be the plague with which the Lord will strike all the people who have gone to war against Jerusalem. Their flesh will rot while they stand on their feet, their eyes will rot in their sockets and their tongue will rot in their mouth.*
>
> Zechariah 14:12

Nuclear, biological and chemical weapons now exist that can cause the terrible afflictions described in this passage.

The Third Temple

What might be the reason for such a multi-national force attacking Jerusalem? One possible (even probable) reason is the building of a third Temple on the Temple Mount. Such a radical architectural move, pioneered not only by orthodox Jews but also by Gentiles who want to see the Temple rebuilt, would certainly be inflammatory, causing a conflagration in the Middle East unlike anything witnessed in Jerusalem since AD 70.

It is interesting to note here that the Bible does seem to indicate that a third Temple might be built. The lengthy visions that Ezekiel had in the 6th century BC (Ezekiel 40-48) are certainly an indicator. The visions he had of the restored Temple go much further than anything witnessed in the second Temple. While some interpret Ezekiel's Temple to be spiritual, there is no reason at all to take his visions as anything other than literal.

This is confirmed even more for us by the fact that the apostle John also appears to have had a vision of a literal, concrete, End Times Temple in Jerusalem:

I was given a reed like a measuring rod and was told, "Go and measure the temple of God and the altar and count the worshipers there. Exclude the outer court. Do not measure it because it has been given to the Gentiles. They will trample on Jerusalem for 42 months. I will give power to my two witnesses and they will prophesy for 1,260 days, clothed in sackcloth."

(Revelation 11:1-3)

John was given instructions to measure the Temple. The Jews have not had a Temple since 70 AD. Plans to build a new Temple are under consideration right now, even as I write this book.

So, to summarise, the Bible prophesies an End Times siege of Jerusalem by an enormous army, perhaps in response to the building of a Third Temple:

The number of the mounted troops was two hundred million. I heard their number.

(Revelation 9:16)

Note that when this prophecy was written, there are thought to have been less than 200 million people on the earth. Dramatic population increases, particularly in the last two hundred years, have made such a large army a possibility.

Once again we see how contemporary this ancient language feels.

The Rise of the Antichrist

The Bible makes it clear that these events will coincide with a figure known as the Antichrist. The word "anti" means "against" and the word "Christ" means "Messiah." The one who is known in the Bible as the Antichrist will be a figure resolutely and defiantly opposed to the view that Jesus is the Messiah, God's Son come to earth and born in human flesh. This Antichrist figure will clearly be someone immensely important and influential on the global, political stage. He will have the capacity to bring billions of people under his spell. He will also commit an act of unprecedented disrespect in and against the sacred place at the historic centre of Israel's life—the Temple, a fact which encourages the view that a literal, third Temple has to be built. As the prophet Daniel foresaw in the time of the Exile of the Jews in Babylon (sixth century BC):

> *He will confirm a covenant with many for seven years. In the middle of the seven years, he will put an end to sacrifice and offering. On a wing, he will set up an abomination that causes desolation until the end that is decreed is poured out on him.*
>
> (Daniel 9:27)

We know more about this figure known as the Antichrist from Biblical prophecy. He will rise to power as a unifying peacemaker. He will help initiate a seven-year peace treaty with Israel and many other countries. However, halfway through the treaty, he will end sacrifices and offerings in the Temple and set up "the abomination that causes desolation". This shows that the rebuilding of the Temple, and the reintroduction of sacrificial offerings, are prerequisites for the fulfilment of this prophecy.

There has been considerable discussion going on for decades about the possibility of rebuilding the Temple and, if and when it happens, it will be of momentous significance. It will set the stage for what the apostle John foresaw in the vision he recorded in Revelation:

> *He opened his mouth to blaspheme God and to slander His name and His dwelling place and those who live in heaven. He was given power to make war against the saints and to conquer them. He was given authority over every tribe, people, language and nation. All inhabitants of the earth will worship the beast, all whose names have not been written in the book of life belonging to the Lamb that was slain from the creation of the world. He who has an ear, let him hear.*
>
> (Revelation 13:6-9)

Profiling the Antichrist

According to Biblical prophecy, the Antichrist will have worldwide control, in some form of "New World Order". All countries of the world will be under his authority. Everyone on the earth will worship him, except those who belong to Christ. It will be like the first century all over again, only it won't be Caesar that people will be worshipping but the Antichrist.

Here it is important to note that there are an increasing number of Christian writers, preachers and thinkers who believe that organizations like the United Nations, the International Monetary Fund, the World Trade Organisation and the World Bank are working towards a "New World Order", at the expense of national sovereignty.

Another interesting facet of this Antichrist's profile is his ability to perform signs that make the peoples of the earth wonder:

> *He performed great and miraculous signs, even causing fire to come down from heaven to earth in full view of people. Because of the signs he was given power to do on behalf of the first beast, he deceived the inhabitants of the earth. He ordered them to set up an image in honour of the beast who was wounded by the*

sword and yet lived. He was given power to give breath to the image of the first beast so that it could speak and cause all who refused to worship the image to be killed. He also forced everyone, small and great, rich and poor, free and slave, to receive a mark in his right hand or in his forehead, so that no one could buy or sell unless he had the mark, which is the name of the beast or the number of his name. This calls for wisdom. If anyone has insight, let them calculate the number of the beast, for it is man's number. His number is 666.

(Revelation 13:13-18)

The Antichrist will perform miracles in public. He will suffer a seemingly fatal wound yet live. He will fool the world.

The Mark of the Beast

According to Revelation 13, everyone will be forced to have a mark on their hand or forehead before being allowed to buy or sell anything. Once again this "mark" seems very relevant in today's world. Imbedded computer chips are a reality; we are on the brink of a cashless society. With the advent of GPS and sophisticated monitoring systems, the technological capability to watch everyone is now a reality too. Notice that it is "the name of the beast or his number", not each individual's name or number. The mark is a mark of allegiance to the "beast"—the demonic global system that will accompany the reign of the Antichrist. Anyone who refuses to worship the beast or receive the mark is likely to be killed. This will certainly include the remnant of faithful Christians on the earth. No one who holds fast to a truly Biblical faith will submit to a system that demands that they break the Commandments.

What happens to those who worship the beast and receive the mark? "If any man worships the beast and his image and receives his mark in his forehead or in his hand, he will drink of the wine of the wrath of God which is poured out in full strength into the cup of his indignation. He shall be tormented with fire and brimstone in the presence of the holy angels and in the presence of the Lamb"

(Revelation 14:9-10). Nobody who worships the beast and receives his mark will be saved.

The Man of Lawlessness

The Antichrist will be known as The Man of Lawlessness. This does not mean that he will advocate that people break the law, in the sense of criminal law. That would create global anarchy and actively contradict his drive for a new world order—an order that will depend 100% on people obeying the laws that the beast (his demonic and oppressive world system) will enshrine. No, this refers to God's Law, to the absolutely binding and eternal Word of God in Scripture. It is this higher Law that the Antichrist will subvert and seek to dishonour and destroy.

The apostle Paul foresaw this clearly in the first century AD. He was writing at a time when Christians were so expectant of the Second Coming of Christ that some were wrongly arguing that it had already happened! Paul quickly put a stop to this eschatological error by pointing to a real event in space and time that must take place before Christ can return. This revolves around the Man of Lawlessness:

> *Concerning the coming of our Lord Jesus Christ, and our being gathered to him, we ask you brothers not to become easily unsettled or alarmed by some prophecy, report or letter supposed to have come from us, saying that the day of the Lord has already come. Don't let anyone deceive you in any way, for that day will not come until the rebellion occurs and the man of lawlessness is revealed, the man doomed to destruction. He will oppose and exalt himself over everything that is called God or that is worshiped. He sets himself up in God's temple, proclaiming himself to be God.*
>
> (2 Thessalonians 2:1-4, written c 50 AD).

The Antichrist will sit in the rebuilt Jewish temple and declare that he is God. This then is the specific act of abomination that causes such great desolation.

The Second Coming

What does Jesus have to say about when He will return?

No one knows about that day or hour, not even the angels in heaven but only the Father. As it was in the days of Noah, so it will be at the coming of the Son of Man.

(Matthew 24:36-37)

Jesus says he will return when the earth is like it was in Noah's day. What was the world like in Noah's day? We have already discussed this in a previous chapter, but let us summarise using words taken from the Biblical story of Noah: "The earth was corrupt before God and it was filled with violence. For God looked upon the earth and it was indeed corrupt. All flesh had corrupted their way upon the earth. God said to Noah, 'The end of all flesh has come before me. The earth is filled with violence through them and I will destroy them with the earth' (Genesis 6:11-13).

If the End Times are going to be like the days of Noah, then they will be terrible indeed. Christians will find it tough to make a stand, yet Jesus exhorts us to be brave and not to compromise. He promises us that He will reward those who persevere under great trial. Indeed, to one of the seven churches in the Book of Revelation, He writes these words:

"Since you have kept my command to endure patiently, I will also keep you from the hour of trial that is going to come upon the whole world to test those who live on the earth. I am coming soon. Hold on to what you have, so that no one will take your crown. I will make the one who overcomes a pillar in the temple of my God. Never again will they leave it. I will write on them the name of my God and the name of the city of my God, the new Jerusalem, which is coming down out of heaven from my God and I will also write on them my new name."

Revelation 3:10-12

If we want to receive this reward we will need to stand firm.

What will happen in these cruel and amoral times? Jesus teaches that these days are going to be so severe for the church that He will lessen the number of days, for the sake of His followers. He says:

> *"If those days had not been cut short, no one would survive, but for the sake of the elect, those days will be shortened. At that time, the sign of the Son of Man will appear in the sky and all the nations of the earth will mourn. They will see the Son of Man coming on the clouds of the sky with power and great glory. He will send his angels with a loud trumpet call and they will gather his elect from the four winds, from one end of the heavens to the other. Heaven and earth will pass away but my words will never pass away. You also must be ready because the Son of Man will come at an hour when you do not expect him."*
>
> (Matthew 24:22, 30-31, 35, 44)

The Son of Man will return with the armies of heaven. This will happen when great tribulation has come against God's people. The exact hour and day will be unknown. Yet there will be signs. In particular, as we saw in a previous chapter, there will be the sign of the blossoming fig tree—the great awakening among the Jewish people who will see that Jesus is their Messiah and Lord:

> *"Look at the fig tree and all the trees. When they sprout leaves, you can see for yourselves and know that summer is near. Even so, when you see these things happening, you know that the kingdom of God is near."*
>
> (Luke 21:29-31).

The Fullness of the Gentiles

It is clear from the above that the exact time of Christ's return is not "revealed knowledge" (some things are hidden and some things are revealed, Deuteronomy 29:29). However, it is also clear that there are things we are supposed to know, a number of "milestones" and pointers that guide our understanding of where we might be on the Biblical timeline.

I want to finish this chapter by considering two further end-times milestones where fulfilment may be imminent.

First, in Matthew 24 Jesus says that the Gospel will be preached to all nations (24:14), before he returns. It seems likely that exponential advances in communications technology in recent years will have brought that goal closer to fulfilment. According to "Ethnologue," the world has 6909 languages and the "Wycliffe Bible Translators" plan to have the Bible, or a part of the Bible, translated into every one of those languages by 2025. At the risk of stating the obvious, we must be much closer to fulfilling the Matthew 24:14 prophecy than ever before!

Secondly, I want to look a little more closely at another aspect of the significance of Israel in End Times prophecy.

The Old Testament is full of promises and prophecies that show that God has a special relationship with Israel and that they would be "the power in the land." However, certainly in worldly terms, Gentiles appear to have taken over the position of favour on the earth.

Prophecy indicates that, in due course, God's relationship with His chosen people will be restored. "Blindness in part is happened to Israel until the fullness of the Gentiles be come in. And so all Israel shall be saved, as it is written" (Romans 11:25, 26, KJV). The expression "until the fullness of the Gentiles has come in" implies a difference between Gentile believers and Israel. It would seem that there is a specific number of Gentile Christians that equates to "fullness."

Christianity is on the increase globally, though we may have difficulty defining what constitutes a Christian and who "is" a Christian. Some consider themselves Christian by birth or nationality, some by church attendance and some by being "born again" (see John 3:3). In truth only God knows who is a committed Christian.

One thing that should challenge all who claim to be a Christian is the Letter sent by the Risen Christ to the church in Laodicea in the

Book of Revelation. Here he addresses a Christian community that is neither hot (on fire for God) nor cold (completely disinterested in God). It is "lukewarm"—characterised by a complacency—that Jesus hates even more than antagonism:

> *"I rebuke and discipline those I love. Be zealous and repent. Here I am! I stand at the door and knock. If anyone hears my voice and opens the door, I will come in and eat with them and they with me. To the one who overcomes, I will give the right to sit with me on my throne, just as I overcame and sat down with my Father on his throne. He who has an ear, let them hear what the Spirit says to the Churches."*
>
> (Revelation 3:19-22)

Over many years the statement, "I stand at the door and knock", has been used by those who have preached the Gospel to those who are not Christians. Usually at the end of a sermon, such preachers interpret the door as the unbeliever's heart. They urge their listeners to open the door to Jesus, who is alive and knocking.

This is a complete misreading of this Scripture!

In its original context, Jesus' invitational appeal was not to non-Christians as individuals but to an entire church community. The door is the door of the local church in question. Jesus says, "If you hear me knocking and let me in, I will restore fellowship with you and you can then move from indifference back to intimacy."

For all of us who claim to be Christians, this prompts a vital question: are we friends with the Risen Jesus?

Further to that, we need to ask: are we prepared to put this friendship first in our lives, even when it costs us dear, as it will in the End Times?

It's clearly a time for getting to know Jesus better.

And where better to start than the Book of Revelation, which is both a vision of what Jesus is really like, and what the church is called to be in the final days of human history?

Chapter 16: AN ENDLESS HOPE

It is truly amazing how the wool is pulled over peoples' eyes about the *Book of Revelation*. It is even more amazing that many of those who tell us to avoid it are the very ones who should be helping and encouraging us to study it!

At its opening in Genesis chapter 1, the Bible quickly moves from the creation of the universe, the earth and human beings to the fall of man and the apparent success of Satan. There follows God's sovereign selection of His chosen people Israel, the story of their triumphs, failures, trials and tribulations, up to the First Coming of Christ. The New Testament describes Jesus' life and role as Redeemer King, including His death, resurrection and ascension to heaven. At the close of the Bible, with the *Book of Revelation* no less, Jesus returns, Satan is overthrown and his followers are defeated. As I have said before, without the *Book of Revelation* the story would be incomplete.

Before considering the structure and objectives of the *Book of Revelation*, I want to emphasise that this has been the subject of much conjecture and debate. Indeed, great tomes have been written on the topic.

It is not my intention to write a detailed commentary on *Revelation* but rather to introduce the subject and to convince you of its importance. For those who wish to read further, David Pawson covers more ground in his *Unlocking the Bible* series, and he recommends George Eldon Ladd's commentary for in-depth study. In subsequent chapters we will be looking in more detail at some End Times indicators and how we might prepare ourselves for what is to come. I hope in the process to instil in you a sense of urgency and a desire to keep watch and speak out so that you will be alert to the "signs of the times" and act as "watch-keepers" and "heralds".

Christ's Magnificent Entrance

Early in Revelation chapter 1 it becomes abundantly clear that God holds the book to be of paramount importance. The author of the book, the apostle John, writing on the Roman penal colony of Patmos, introduces his visions with the following words:

> *The revelation from Jesus Christ, which God gave him to show his servants what must soon take place. He made it known by sending his angel to his servant John...*

Who gave what to whom? A superficial study might suggest that the revelation was given to John, and in a way it was. However, it is more accurate to say that the revelation was given to Jesus by God the Father and witnessed by John. Some scholars believe the word "soon" should be interpreted as "over a short space of time", rather than "in the near future"

> *John, who testifies to everything he saw—that is, the word of God and the testimony of Jesus Christ.*

Jesus revealed the testimony to John in a vision sequence during which John watched the events and was directed to write them down.

> *Blessed is the one who reads aloud the words of this prophecy, and blessed are those who hear it and take to heart what is written in it, because the time is near.*

There can be no doubt from these words that *The Book of Revelation* comes under the category of prophecy; after all, it says so! It is the only book in the Bible that specifically says that it blesses the reader, and the hearer who takes it to heart.

> *John, To the seven churches in the province of Asia: Grace and peace to you from him who is, and who was, and who is to come, and from the seven spirits before his throne...*

Asia was a province of the Roman Empire (what we would now know as part of Turkey).

Grace is a free gift that we do not deserve and cannot earn. It is from Jesus "who is, and who was, and who is to come". Peace is the outcome or by-product of grace—peace with God, peace with one another, peace within, and peace with our environment.

Notice how at the start of *The Book of Revelation* John is instructed to send letters from the Risen Jesus to seven churches. The number seven is very important to John in both his Gospel (where there are, for example, seven "I am" sayings of Jesus) and in Revelation. In the latter there are numerous "7s": 7 churches, 7 lampstands, 7 trumpets, 7 seals, 7 bowls, 7 stars, and there are many more.

Seven is a very important number in Judaism. To the Jewish mind it is symbolic of perfection.

> *... and from Jesus Christ, who is the faithful witness, the firstborn from the dead, and the ruler of the kings of the earth. To him who loves us and has freed us from our sins by his blood...*

Remember that the word "revelation" means literally "unveiling." When a famous person in history is commemorated, a statue is often made of them and erected in a strategic location in a major metropolis. When it is time for the hero in question to be celebrated, the statue is unveiled and the public see a replica of their national hero.

This is in effect what happens in the *Book of Revelation*. Through his visions, John artistically unveils the glory of the greatest human being that has ever graced the stage of history—Jesus of Nazareth. Just in the above verse alone, John celebrates the fact that Jesus is (1) the faithful witness, (2) the firstborn from the dead, (3) the ruler of the kings of the earth, (4) the one who loves us, (5) and the one who has freed us from our sins by his blood (in other words, our Saviour).

But notice this. John is not unveiling a dead hero. Jesus is "the firstborn from the dead." He is the first of millions, billions even, who will live forever. Unlike all the other heroes in history, who were alive but are now dead, Jesus was dead but is now alive for evermore. That marks him out as unique in the whole sweep of human history. The unveiling of Jesus in Revelation is the unveiling of the Resurrected and Ascended One.

> *... and has made us to be a kingdom and priests to serve his God and Father—to him be glory and power for ever and ever! Amen.*

Here John is told the purpose of why Jesus came—to make us a kingdom of priests. This had always been Israel's destiny (see Exodus 19:1-5). Priests are those who draw near to God. Intimacy is their destiny. Those who follow Jesus will become the royal friends of God.

> *Look, he is coming with the clouds, and every eye will see him, even those who pierced him; and all peoples on earth will mourn because of him. So shall it be! Amen.*

The overall theme of The Book of Revelation is simply this: that the Lord Jesus Christ is coming back to earth with the clouds—the great manifestation of the glory of God. Everyone alive on the globe will see him. There will be no mistaking what is happening and who is coming when Christ returns. There will be great and godly sorrow all over the planet when people see the final great unveiling of Christ when He comes again. They will realise in despair and agony of soul that they neglected and rejected the Lord of history and the Saviour of their sins.

> *"I am the Alpha and the Omega," says the Lord God, "who is, and who was, and who is to come, the Almighty."*

Alpha and omega are the first and last letters of the Greek alphabet (the language in which the New Testament was originally written). God is the beginning and the end of all things, including human history. He started everything at Creation and He will complete everything at the end of time. While the unbeliever says, "I don't know what the world is coming to," the believer says, "I know who's coming to the world."

I, John, your brother and companion in the suffering and kingdom and patient endurance that are ours in Jesus, was on the island of Patmos because of the word of God and the testimony of Jesus.

John shows, from both his exile and endurance, that following Jesus is not always an easy road. The way can be full of suffering which is why Jesus told His followers to take up their cross. During the End Times, the path will be full of persecution and hardship. Just as the Roman Empire oppressed John, so the "one world order"—with its insistence that all citizens of the earth bear the mark of the beast—will oppress the true lovers of God in the End Times.

On the Lord's Day I was in the Spirit, and I heard behind me a loud voice like a trumpet...

One possible interpretation of "the Lord's day" is that this was the day once a year when every citizen in the Roman Empire had to go to a public place, burn incense in a pagan ceremony, and confess that Caesar (the Roman Emperor) was dominus, namely "lord." This was a challenge to any genuine Christian because in the New Testament Christ is Lord, not Caesar. So it may have been on this day, when Roman citizens throughout the Empire were declaring that a man in Rome was divine, that John saw the supremacy and authority of Jesus Christ.

... which said: "Write on a scroll what you see and send it to the seven churches: to Ephesus, Smyrna, Pergamum, Thyatira, Sardis, Philadelphia and Laodicea."

The seven churches mentioned here were local churches in the first century. You can still visit the sites of the cities where they were based in modern Turkey. Notice how the first church to be mentioned is Ephesus. This may well have been the "mother church"—the apostolic base from which the other six were planted.

The words that the Risen Jesus spoke to these churches are as relevant to churches in the twenty first century as they were in the first. After two thousand years of history, they still have the power to penetrate through our religious defences and challenge us to restore our first love for Jesus, which is what He asks the church in Ephesus to do. The priority of all believers is to keep drawing near to the Father, as kingdom priests, and to cherish friendship with Jesus above all other things.

> *I turned around to see the voice that was speaking to me. And when I turned I saw seven golden lampstands…*

John turns round to see a voice! That strange sentence should capture our imaginations! Normally you hear a voice. But this Voice is the Voice of the Lord. This is Jesus, whom John in the opening of his gospel calls "the Word." Jesus Christ is the Father's complete and exhaustive word to human beings. If we ignore the Voice, we will find ourselves in a perilous predicament in the Age to Come.

> *… and among the lampstands was someone like a son of man, dressed in a robe reaching down to his feet and with a golden sash around his chest.*

Notice that the Voice—namely Jesus—is standing among the seven lampstands. There's the number seven again. The lampstands are the seven-branched candlesticks that used to adorn the Jewish Temple. They are known as *menorhot* (*menorah* in the singular). Each of the seven churches in Asia Minor had a menorah in heaven and Jesus, dressed here as a great high priest, tends these lampstands.

To every church the call is the same: we must keep the fire of love for God burning on the altar of our hearts, come what may.

> *The hair on his head was white like wool, as white as snow, and his eyes were like blazing fire.*

White hair represents wisdom and eyes like blazing fire symbolises judgement (see also, Daniel 7:9).

His feet were like bronze glowing in a furnace, and his voice was like the sound of rushing waters.

Notice two things about John's description of the Risen Jesus here.

First, Jesus is portrayed in language that would have reminded his original hearers of the Roman Emperor. Only in this case, Jesus is clearly far superior in appearance, authority and aura to all the Emperors in history put together.

Second, to emphasize the point, John hints at the imperfection of these Emperors and the perfection of Jesus by naming seven qualities in his portrayal of Jesus.

This becomes very clear if we add the next verse and then count up the number of features that John describes in his unveiling of the Risen and Ascended Lord Jesus:

In his right hand he held seven stars, and coming out of his mouth was a sharp, double-edged sword. His face was like the sun shining in all its brilliance.

This verse completes the portrait and the list of details:

His hair – white as wool

His eyes – blazing with fire

His feet – burnished with bronze

His voice – as thunderous as the waters of the sea

His right hand – holding seven stars

His mouth – issuing a sharp sword

His face – shining as the sun

John, a friend of Jesus, is now seeing Jesus as he has never been seen before, in His full ascended heavenly glory. Jesus is indeed King of kings and Lord of lords.

When I saw him, I fell at his feet as though dead. Then he placed his right hand on me and said: "Do not be afraid. I am the First and the Last...."

The glory, magnificence and splendour of Jesus are altogether beyond our comprehension. When we are given a revelation of the heavenly majesty of Jesus, it can quite literally floor us.

I am the Living One; I was dead, and now look, I am alive for ever and ever! And I hold the keys of death and Hades.

Jesus holds the keys that can set us free. He has the power and authority to grant us eternal life so that death has no hold over us. If we put our life in His hands, by faith we are saved and by grace we are delivered from the consequences of sin.

Write, therefore, what you have seen, what is now and what will take place later.

John is directed to write down his visions of present history (especially the seven churches) and future history (the End Times).

The mystery of the seven stars that you saw in my right hand and of the seven golden lampstands is this: The seven stars are the angels of the seven churches, and the seven lampstands are the seven churches.

Jesus gives John some vital keys to understanding the symbolism of heaven. The seven stars that the Risen Lord holds in His right hand are seven angels—one for each of the seven churches that receive letters from Him in chapters two and three of *The Book of Revelation.*

Isn't it a comfort to know that every local church has an angel assigned to it?

The seven lampstands are the seven churches.

Isn't it a comfort to know that Jesus himself watches over each church?

See how every verse of the opening of *The Book of Revelation* could itself be the subject of a book! I commend the entire book to you as worthy of careful study.

God wants us to know how the story of history will conclude. He wants us to know what to expect.

God wants every Christian to know that death does not mark a hopeless end. It is the doorway to an endless hope.

In the next chapter, we will follow John through the door that opens up to him in the heavenly realms and catch a glimpse of the hope that is to come for every true follower of Jesus.

Chapter 17: THE SHAPE OF THINGS TO COME

The *Book of Revelation* is a difficult read and we all need help. However, the fundamental point is simple: thanks to *Revelation*, we know how the book of history ends.

Jesus wins!

You may ask why we aren't focusing on other sections of the Bible in the fourth part of my book. I should make it clear that for a full appreciation of End Times prophecy it is necessary to study a wide range of Old Testament prophetic books and New Testament Scriptures, some of which we have looked at in earlier chapters. The reason why *Revelation* is such a vital book is because it provides the final drawing together of the End Time prophetic writings. For example, the description of the Antichrist, given in Daniel 9, is developed more fully in Revelation 13. Similarly, the End Times material in Daniel 7-12, Isaiah 24-27, Ezekiel 37-41 and Zechariah 9-12 are all given a fuller treatment in *Revelation*. This shows how *Revelation* cannot be studied in isolation. Some go so far as to suggest that the whole Bible could be studied through the lenses of the *Book of Revelation,* to which I would comment that such an undertaking would not be for the fainthearted!

Revelation 1-3

In the last chapter we effectively covered chapters 1-3 of *Revelation*. Chapter 1 presents John's vision of the Risen Lord in heaven, standing among the seven lampstands, representing seven local churches in Asia Minor. In chapters 2 and 3, Jesus dictates a letter to each of these churches and John, acting as a kind of heavenly secretary, faithfully records the revelation and then sends it to the angel of each church.

Some have suggested that the angels in question were in reality the senior pastors of these first century congregations.

However angelic vicars and ministers can sometimes be, I don't think that this is the correct interpretation!

These angels were angels!

What then are these letters about?

The letters are written to churches with very different stories and settings: Ephesus, Smyrna, Pergamum, Thyatira, Sardis, Philadelphia and Laodicea. They summarise positive and negative aspects of these congregations. Where Jesus sees negative traits through his eyes that blaze with fire, he provides loving words of rebuke. Where he sees positive traits, he affirms and applauds the believers in the church in question.

Remember: it was tough being a follower of Jesus in the first century. Christians were required to declare that Caesar is lord. Many refused and were either imprisoned or impoverished as a result. Some were even put to death. Jesus is therefore trying to encourage every believer in all seven churches to be exactly what he is: a "faithful witness."

The pattern of the letters is fairly consistent. Each is addressed to a specific church, followed by a celebration of a particular characteristic of Jesus. Then comes positive comments (although there are none for the churches in Sardis or Laodicea) and negative comments (there are none for the churches in Smyrna or Philadelphia), and advice to each. The letters close with an entreaty that the readers will open their ears and hear, and with a specific promise of reward for faithfulness, which is different for each church.

These letters are relatively straightforward and understandable (which is not to say that we don't need to work at interpreting some of the symbolism in them). They are easy to grasp compared to the chapters that follow.

Revelation 4-22

From chapter 4 onwards we move into an altogether more challenging series of visions that are filled with the kind of symbolism, allegory and metaphor that is common to ancient apocalyptic literature (literature in which Jewish mystics had purported visions of the end of all things) but which is not so common to our eyes and ears today. Students who want to capture an accurate understanding of what John meant in his original, first century setting, need to become familiar not only with the symbolism of the Old Testament but with the symbolism of the Roman Empire that had imprisoned him.

That is a tall order even for the finest minds!

If the symbolism of the language can be quite elusive, so is the structure of the book as a whole. Some scholars argue that there are seven visions in Revelation 4-22, each of which is linked to a matching day in the seven days of creation as described in Genesis 1. They suggest in other words that the order of events links the beginning with the end. This is a very common pattern in literary writing. It is known as *inclusio* (the ancient Roman term) or "ring composition." This is used by authors who want the end of their books or speeches to return to themes raised right at the beginning.

It would be quite natural for John to have done this.

Bible scholar Charles Talbert has identified the seven visions of the End Times in Revelation 4-19 as follows:

4:1 - 8:1: The Seven Seals

8:2 - 11:18: The Seven Trumpets

11:19 - 13:18: The Roots and Role of Roman Power

14:1 - 20:	The Seven Agents of Judgment
15:1 - 16:21:	The Seven Plagues of Wrath
17:1 - 19:5:	The Role and Results of Imperial Power
19:6 - 22:5:	The Consummation

However it should be noted that there seemingly as many views of the structure of Revelation 4-22 as there are scholars!

The same is true for the timeline and sequence of events described in the book. Here again there are countless and often confusing interpretations. Many scholars have a preconceived idea of how the End Times is going to pan out and then force the passages of the Book of Revelation into confirming their particular theology. This can lead to quite bewildering contortions of the text and the provision of flow charts that would test some of the finest mathematicians and statisticians on the planet!

Perhaps one of the simplest and clearest explanations of the order of these chapters of the main body of *The Book of Revelation* has been provided by Bible teacher David Pawson:

Part 1 (Heaven: "Up There")

Revelation 4-5:

IN HEAVEN, THINGS ARE ALL RIGHT

Part 2 (Earth: "Down Here")

Revelation 6-19:

ON EARTH, THINGS WILL GET MUCH WORSE BEFORE THEY GET BETTER

Part 3 (Heaven: "Down Here", because heaven comes to earth)

Revelation 20-22

THINGS WILL GET MUCH BETTER AFTER THEY HAVE GOT MUCH WORSE

The key to this sequence is the pivotal turning point of the entire book: the return of Jesus Christ in chapter 19. This is the event that causes history to change direction from rubble to redemption and from violence to victory. The Second Coming of Christ brings heaven to earth, quite literally.

All this shows that while Revelation 1-3 deals with the present (the state of the seven churches at the time that John was writing), Revelation 4-22 describes the future (the End Times). The exact order of events in the future is not easy to pin down. I have the impression that John, who is acting as scribe in Revelation, is seeing visions on a huge scale (like vast paintings) and trying to scribble down what catches his eye, without necessarily having time to arrange and classify the information in exact chronological order. It is clear that there are two or three sections that are digressions or parentheses from the central narrative. Furthermore, the unusual style, which is not in character with John's other writings (as in his Gospel), may have remained "unedited" because of the very strong warning against alteration that is given in 22:18-19. These verses show us again that Revelation is both unique and of huge significance; no other book of the Bible has such a "health warning"

What is abundantly clear is the fact that Revelation is the final Biblical warning that the world as we know it will end and there will be judgement. In simple terms, it shows that:

- Things on earth are not right and the church is not as it should be (chapters 2-3)
- Things in heaven are right and as they should be: God is on His throne, as He has been throughout history, and Jesus is the overseer and leader for the end time plan and action (4-5)
- Things will deteriorate and the world will suffer great tribulation and woe for 3½ years under the leadership of the unholy trinity of Satan, the Antichrist and the False Prophet (6-18)
- Things will get much better; Jesus will return as King of kings and Lord of lords, defeat the armies of the unholy trinity and

> then establish his rule on the earth for a thousand years. The Day of Judgement will be at the end of the millennium rule, followed by the ushering in of the new heaven and earth and the New Jerusalem (Ch. 19-22).

As I said at the start of this chapter, the central message of the *Book of Revelation* is that Jesus wins!

But if he wins, that must mean that he wins against someone or something.

So who is Jesus' opponent in *Revelation?*

Chapter 18: THE COUNTERFEIT CHRIST

As I have intimated in earlier chapters, God has provided us with all the information we need concerning the future. This includes the battle plans of the Antichrist, manifested in the systems and laws that are evident all around us in the world today. God has done His part in warning us what is to come. We must do our part in searching the Scriptures and studying the signs of the times, acting on our findings in any way that seems appropriate to the insight concerned. That might mean in some cases writing to the Press, to your MP, talking to people, speaking at public meetings, supporting others who do these things, or even writing a book!

The key thing here is to obey the old adage: KNOW YOUR ENEMY.

We need to know what the Bible teaches about those who will arise in the End Times to oppose God and His people. We need not only to build a clear picture of what the enemy looks like but also what his plans are.

We are not to be ignorant of our enemy's schemes and strategies.

Forewarned is definitely forearmed.

In this chapter I therefore want to look at what the Bible teaches about the Antichrist and the signs that help us identify him.

The Three Kinds of Antichrist

Christ is the "anointed one", the Messiah. In the Greek language of the New Testament, "anti" means both against and a replacement for, so the antichrist opposes and seeks to usurp Christ.

We see from 1 John 2:18-23 and 4:3 that there are at least three kinds of antichrist to consider. There are "antichrists" who are false teachers, some of whom pretend to be Christians. They lead people astray by denying that the human Jesus was the divinely appointed Messiah. They teach that the Christ has not come to earth in the flesh and are therefore in a very real sense anti-Christ. It seems from 1 John 2 that antichrists are sometimes present in, and will go out from, the church ("they went out from us," v.19). The "badges" of their true identity will be their denial that Jesus is the Son of God (22-23) and that Christ came to us "in the flesh" (4:1-3).

Then secondly there is "the spirit of antichrist". This is a spirit of deception because it turns Jesus into a spiritual Christ—one in which Jesus is not the Christ from his conception to his crucifixion. Such a spiritualised Christ undermines the Incarnation—the view that Christ came to us in human flesh and that he is fully Man as well as fully God.

Thirdly there is "the Antichrist" who will rise to power in the last days—an actual figure on the stage of history who is the epitome of everything that John meant by the antichrist teachers of his own time and the embodiment of the spirit of antichrist that has deceived people throughout the ages (including our own) into describing Jesus as the Heavenly Christ while denying that he was, two thousand years ago, the earthly Christ.

In addition to these three there is also a possible fourth. In chapter 11, we looked at the End Times passage that talks about things happening "until the full number of the gentiles has come in" (Romans 11:25). I may be being slightly whimsical here but imagine that there is some kind of meter or counter in heaven clocking up the number of Gentiles coming to believe in Jesus. At some point this counter or clock will reach the "full" preordained figure. Satan, I am sure, knows this but and I am also sure that he cannot tell when the "full number" will occur. He is not given access to that kind of detail. In such circumstances, isn't it reasonable to suppose that he is compelled to have an Antichrist ready in the wings (or even on stage) throughout history? Perhaps this is why some of the tyrants of history—such as Adolf Hitler—were antichrist in spirit and so like the portrait of the Antichrist in the Bible. This we could therefore describe as a contingency anti-Christ.

A Counterfeiter Comes

The rise of the End Times Antichrist (the third sense above) is outlined by Paul in 2 Thessalonians 2:1-12:

Concerning the coming of our Lord Jesus Christ and our being gathered to him, we ask you, brothers and sisters, not to become easily unsettled or alarmed by the teaching allegedly from us—whether by a prophecy or by word of mouth or by letter—asserting that the day of the Lord has already come.

It seems that there had been rumours, or a letter purporting to come from Paul, that led the Thessalonians to think they had somehow missed the return of Christ. Paul takes the opportunity to describe some fundamental prerequisites concerning "the day of the Lord:"

Don't let anyone deceive you in any way, for that day will not come until the rebellion occurs and the man of lawlessness is revealed, the man doomed to destruction.

Paul clearly warns his readers that if the Antichrist has not been revealed in history then Jesus has not yet returned. This arrival or appearance of the Antichrist will be preceded and accompanied by what Paul calls "the rebellion"—which may refer to a great apostasy, a falling away from the Christian faith, or to the proliferation of false teaching.

He will oppose and will exalt himself over everything that is called God or is worshiped, so that he sets himself up in God's temple, proclaiming himself to be God. Don't you remember that when I was with you I used to tell you these things?

The Antichrist will oppose God, claim to be God, and take God's seat in the Temple. It is interesting to note that the church at Thessalonica was planted in about AD 50 and both letters (1 and 2 Thessalonians) were written shortly thereafter, in about 51 AD. That means that the new Christians in Thessalonica were taught about the End Times from the very start of their journey of faith. How different it is in churches today! If the End Times are addressed at all in public preaching (which they rarely are in many contexts outside the USA), then the subject is usually regarded as too demanding for young Christians and reserved for those who want meatier teaching on the faith. This is quite the opposite of Paul's approach. He taught new converts about the End Times from the earliest moment, including teaching about the Antichrist:

And now you know what is holding him back, so that he may be revealed at the proper time. For the secret power of lawlessness is already at work; but the one who now holds it back will continue to do so till he is taken out of the way

Paul teaches that there is a restraining power holding the Antichrist back from appearing on the stage of history. This restraining power will one day be withdrawn. Who or what is this restraining power? It is thought by some to be the Holy Spirit and by others to be the church. When this power is withdrawn by God, the Antichrist will emerge. If this power is the church, then this suggests that the church may be spared the great tribulation and will experience what is called the Rapture (God snatching Christians out of the world before the big trouble starts). If it means the Holy Spirit, which seems to be the best interpretation of the text, then it indicates that God will remove his protective presence from the world and allow Satan to unleash hell on earth. This will lead to the appearance of the Antichrist, whom Paul here also refers to as the Man of Lawlessness:

And then the lawless one will be revealed, whom the Lord Jesus will overthrow with the breath of his mouth and destroy by the splendour of his coming.

While Jesus will eventually appear to conquer the Antichrist, there will be a period of time in which the Antichrist will hold power, deceiving people by the use of false wonders.

The coming of the lawless one will be in accordance with how Satan works. He will use all sorts of displays of power through signs and wonders that serve the lie...

The Antichrist will perform what look like miracles in order to boost the authority and credibility of his claims. These will not be true signs and wonders but demonic counterfeits. They will be like those performed in Pharaoh's court in the time of Moses. The court magicians there were sorcerers who sought to mimic the true miracles performed by Moses. The Antichrist will perform the same kinds of tricks.

And all the ways that wickedness deceives those who are perishing. They perish because they refused to love the truth and so be saved. For this reason God sends them a powerful delusion so that they will believe the lie and so that all will be condemned who have not believed the truth but have delighted in wickedness.

In order to be able to protect ourselves and stand firm against deception we need to study the Word of God (the Bible) and know the truth. We must test all things and if they are not Biblically sound and do not point to Jesus, we must not compromise by putting our faith in whatever is being advocated, however reasonable it may appear.

A Counterfeit Trinity

The sequence of events relating to the emergence of the Antichrist on the world's stage is described metaphorically in Revelation 13. Satan's (the dragon's) Antichrist is the beast from the sea (v.1) given Satan's power and throne (v.2). We have discussed the whereabouts of "Satan's throne" earlier in the book and it may be that the Antichrist will first become apparent in Pergamum or perhaps, Berlin. The beast appears to have recovered from a fatal wound (v.3) and the world is amazed and worships Satan and the beast (v4).

The beast holds power for 42 months (v.5), blasphemes against God (v.6) overcomes the saints (v.7) and is given authority over all peoples, except those whose names are in the Book of Life (v.8). This calls for the steadfast endurance of the saints (vv.9-10).

There is another beast (v.11) called the false prophet in Revelation 19:20, whose role is to direct the worship of the peoples of the earth to the first beast (v12). This second beast performs great miracles. He deceives the people and orders them to make an image of the first beast, to which he then gives breath so that it can speak. All who refuse to worship the image are put to death (v13-15).

To show their allegiance, and in order to buy or sell, people are required, on pain of death, to have a mark on their forehead or right hand (vv.16-17).

The last verse of the chapter refers to the number of the beast (666), which has given rise to much speculation and numerical gymnastics. The verse itself advises the application of spiritual wisdom and insight in calculating—which I take to mean in interpreting the number. One key may lie in remembering that seven is the perfect number in Judaism. The number six, on the other hand, is often associated with imperfection and evil.

How does this help us? Revelation 13 shows that there is a hellish counterfeit nature of the Heavenly Trinity—Satan (the dragon), the first beast (the Antichrist) and the second beast (the false prophet). This counterfeit Trinity seeks to replace God the Father, God the Son and God the Holy Spirit.

If this is the case, then the Trinity in heaven would be characterised by the three numbers denoting perfection: 777.

The Trinity in hell, on the other hand, would be characterised by the three numbers denoting imperfection and evil: 666. This unholy trinity is made up of Satan, the Antichrist, and the False Prophet.

A Counterfeit Resurrection

Revelation 13 is written in the common prophetic style of a writer who is witnessing, or appears to be involved in, current events. One of these events seems to surround a fatal wound inflicted on the Antichrist—a wound from which he miraculously recovers (a demonic mimicking of the Resurrection of Christ). There is a Scripture, Zechariah 11:17, which some scholars believe describes the Antichrist and his wounding:

> *"Woe to the worthless shepherd,*
> *who deserts the flock!*
> *May the sword strike his arm and his right eye!*
> *May his arm be completely withered,*
> *his right eye totally blinded!"*

This wounding may lie behind the Antichrist's insistence that everyone who obeys him should have a mark on their bodies. The mark of allegiance on peoples' foreheads or hand may be a way of getting the Antichrist's followers to identify with his wound. The Antichrist will, after all, be a deceiver and a manipulator. He will be viewed as a hero and as a peacemaker. In reality, he will be the very opposite of Jesus Christ, as we will see in the next chapter.

Chapter 19: BEHOLD THE LAMB!

***The Book of Revelation* could have been entitled "The Last Battle." Many of the greatest stories ever written conclude with a final and ferocious contest between the forces of good and evil. The Bible is no exception. Covering the great sweep of human history, the Bible comes to a dramatic and cosmic finale with Revelation—a book that pits the Christ of heaven against the Antichrist on earth, the light of God's glory against the pitch black darkness of hell. At the same time the great difference between this story and the epic stories that are authored by human beings alone is that this story is history. It may be in the future, but the *Book of Revelation* does not describe a fantastic or mythical world. No, this is the furthest remove from fiction. The *Book of Revelation* describes the final facts of planet earth. It portrays what must come in the days, months and years ahead.**

As in all the great stories, at the heart of the battle is a protagonist (the hero or lead character) facing a wicked and sinister antagonist (the villain). The hero is Jesus Christ, described some 28 times in Revelation as the Lamb (of God). The antagonist is the Antichrist, referred to some 30 times as the beast, or the wild beast. The Lamb and the beast are polar opposites.

The Lamb is pure, selfless and just. His virtues are beyond number or compare. Jesus is purity personified. He is the very epitome of mercy and love. He is omniscient and omnipotent. He is God Almighty.

The beast is a domineering, controlling, lying, vicious, arrogant, murderous and selfish despot.

Who will you follow?

Answering that question will not only determine whether you align with darkness or light in the End Times.

It will decide your eternal destiny.

Decision Time

At the time of Christ's First Coming, people had to make a decision whether or not to follow Him. As we prepare for his Second Coming, billions of people will need to choose where to place their allegiance.

Two thousand years ago a great crowd gathered outside the Praetorium in Jerusalem. This was the palatial residence of the Roman governor Pontius Pilate. Pilate was faced with a decision. Would he condemn Jesus to death or set Him free?

Pilate knew that Jesus was an innocent man. He had been brought before him by the Jewish leaders in Jerusalem—religious leaders who were determined to have Jesus crucified. These leaders insisted that Pilate put Jesus to death.

Pilate tried to sit on the fence. He had Jesus flogged to try and appease the blood lust of the Jewish elders but this only seemed to make them even more insistent on the death sentence. Pilate put the issue to the crowds in the hope that they would see reason.

He had two men brought before the masses, only one of whom could be released. Barabbas stood to one side, a violent insurrectionist arrested during the Passover. Jesus, beaten and bruised, stood the other. Faced with this choice, the crowds pointed to Jesus and shouted "Crucify him!"

Pilate's hand was now forced. Neutrality was impossible. In trying not to make a decision it turned out that he had made his decision.

And so Jesus was led to the Cross, like a lamb to the slaughter (just as the prophet had predicted in Isaiah 53). On the same day that the Passover lambs were being slaughtered in the Temple in the city, the Lamb of God was slain outside the city on a hill known as the Place of the Skull.

As John the Baptist declared three years before this terrible moment, "Behold, the Lamb of God who takes away the sin of the world!"

Pilate's example is a lesson to all of us. In the end, everyone will need to decide whether to follow Christ or the world. Neutrality for us will turn out to be impossible too. If we are entering into or living in the dark days known as the End Times, then we will not be able to remain indifferent or undecided. Sooner or later, like Pilate, our hands will be forced. We will have to make a choice. Will we come under the tyrannical control of the beast or the loving lordship of the Lamb?

If you are not yet a Christian, now would be a good time to make a decision to follow Christ. Whom would you rather serve? The one who became a victim in order that you could be free (the Lamb), or the one who turns people into victims, in order that they will lose their freedom (the beast)?

Don't conform to the crowds, as so many did at Christ's First Coming. Resist the herd instinct and dare to be different, to be radical, to follow the Lamb not the beast.

If you are already a Christian, now would be a good time to make sure that you are living as a faithful follower of Jesus. One of the invitations that Jesus gives us in the Book of Revelation is this: "Be faithful even to death and I will give you the crown of everlasting life."

Jesus wants a church full of faithful people. He doesn't necessarily want huge churches. He would rather have congregations that are faithful and few than ones that are loveless and large.

If you are not part of a church, find one where Jesus Christ, the

Lamb of God, is clearly the centre of everything.

Find a congregation where the Holy Spirit is clearly present, for where the Holy Spirit remains, there the Lamb reigns!

The First and Second Coming

Why is it so important to emphasize the need to make a decision? There are two answers to this question. The first has to do with the *nature* of Jesus' Second Coming, the second His *purpose.*

When Jesus returns to planet earth, it will be a surprise to the vast majority of people. The Greek word most commonly used to describe his return is *Parousia.* This word was used for the sudden appearance of a man of great influence, usually a king or a general. In the Roman Empire it was used for the unexpected visitation of the most powerful man in the world, the Emperor. If Caesar paid an unanticipated visit to a city such as Pergamum, then the citizens of that city would have described it as a *Parousia.* There would be widespread commotion as people everywhere pushed to see the Emperor, shouting *Parousia! Parousia!*

This is the word that the New Testament writers use of the Second Coming of Christ. That too will be a Parousia. It will take the vast majority of people by surprise. Only a few will be ready. The rest will have their mouths open in awe and their legs will be trembling.

Why will they be in awe? It is because the man at the head of His heavenly entourage will be greater than any monarch who has ever reigned, any emperor who has ever ruled, any president who has ever held office, and any prime minister who has ever led a country.

All such governors, rulers and leaders will in fact lay their crowns before this man and call him "King of kings and Lord of lords!"

This man, returning on the clouds with armies of angels, is none other than Jesus.

As at the First Coming, we will "Behold the Lamb!"

So the first reason why it's important to make a decision is because Christ's return will be sudden. It will catch the vast majority of people off guard. It stands to reason then that it would be better to make a decision now while there's still time than then, when it will be too late.

The second reason has to do with the purpose of Christ's Second Coming.

If we want to see the purpose of Christ's First Coming, we need look no further than His first sermon, preached in His own home town, at the synagogue in Nazareth. He read from the liturgical reading for the day, Isaiah chapter 61. Taking hold of the ancient scroll, He began to declare the words uttered 600 years before—words that were in fact about Him:

The Spirit of the Sovereign LORD is on me,
because the LORD has anointed me
to proclaim good news to the poor.
He has sent me to bind up the broken-hearted,
to proclaim freedom for the captives
and release from darkness for the prisoners,
to proclaim the year of the LORD's favour,

The odd thing is (or is it odd?) Jesus stopped reading at a comma and rolled up the scroll.

Notice the note of mercy. Using Isaiah's words, Jesus announces that He has come to bring hope to the poor and healing to the sick. He has come to bring comfort to the bereaved and freedom to the captives. He has come to usher in God's Jubilee—an extended year of favour (two thousand years, no less) in which God gives a season of grace in which millions will turn back to Him and love Him because of what Jesus has done.

But then look at what Jesus does not say. He does not read the verses from Isaiah 61 that follow.

Here they are, and they strike a very different note:

and the day of vengeance of our God,
to comfort all who mourn,
and provide for those who grieve in Zion—
to bestow on them a crown of beauty
instead of ashes,
the oil of joy
instead of mourning,
and a garment of praise
instead of a spirit of despair.

If the first quotation strikes a note of mercy, these words strike a note of judgment. One day God is going to reap revenge on those who have oppressed His people. Those who grieve in Zion, His chosen people (the faithful remnant of the Jewish people and Gentiles who have chosen to follow Jesus) will see "the wrath of the Lamb"—a wrath that will cause even the unbelieving leaders of the nations to run and hide, a wrath that will bring comfort to all those whose mothers and fathers, sons and daughters, brothers and sisters, have been tortured and slaughtered by the beast and those who have foolishly bowed down to him.

You see the point? Christ's First Coming was all about mercy and salvation. His Second Coming will be all about wrath and judgment.

Given that Christ's return will be both sudden and stern, it would be wise to make a decision to believe in Him now. When we put our trust in the Lamb of God, His blood, which He shed for us, covers us and protects us against the wrath to come.

The Urgency of the Hour

I hope from what I have written that you are convinced by now that studying Biblical prophecy is not only important, it is urgent. Knowing the signs of the End Times is not just a matter of academic interest. It is a matter of life and death.

I hear many Christians today who give little credence to Biblical prophecy, saying that it is all too difficult, allegorical or "spiritualised", and full of "doom and gloom". My answer is that it is real, accurate and far too important to ignore. Ignorance is not bliss; it is hazardous in the extreme. To ignore the signposts that God has given us, as "a light shining in a dark place" (2 Peter 1:19), is to put our eternal wellbeing in jeopardy.

The message of Biblical prophecy is clear; the day of judgement is yet to come and when Jesus returns the righteous will be redeemed and the "free choice" option will end.

In my view much of the world is in disarray and the prevailing mood is one of uncertainty and apprehension. The efforts of man to bring order and sense to the world are not proving effective. I am convinced that redemption and restoration will only be achieved when Jesus returns.

What then are we to expect before Christ comes back?

What signs are there that his *Parousia* is near?

And what evidence is there of such signs in the world today?

I will attempt to answer these questions in Part 5.

Part 5: WHAT NEXT?

Chapter 20: IS IT SOON?

In this chapter I want to give a brief overview of some key End Time (or Second Advent) signs and prophecies in sequence. I hope that an awareness of these signs will help us to see if any world events, as they unfold in the weeks, months and years ahead, can honestly be described as fulfilling Biblical prophecy. I want to avoid "conspiracy theories" or trying to adjust the facts to confirm a hypothesis. At the same time, I wouldn't want to miss things that have genuine spiritual significance and which can be shown as proof of prophetic fulfilment to a sceptical world.

Past, Present and Future Signs

I mention first some things that seem particularly significant in light of current events. These are events prophesied in the Bible and which seem to have particular relevance in light of what is occurring in the world today, especially in the Middle East. These are all prophecies that need to be borne in mind by anyone who is intentional about marrying past prophecies with contemporary occurrences. They are, in short, signs of the End Times:

- Egyptian will turn against Egyptian (Isaiah 19:2)
- Damascus will be in ruins (Isaiah 17:1)
- Gaza will writhe in agony (Zechariah 9:5)
- There will be false teachers and prophets who lead people astray (2 Peter 2:1-2)

- Earthquakes, famines, plague and pestilences will intensify (Luke 21:11)
- Travel and knowledge will increase greatly (Daniel 12:4)
- People will prefer fantasy to reality, myth to Christian truths (2 Timothy 4:3-4).

All these are signs to observe and study.

At the same time we can categorise other signs under three headings, roughly corresponding to past, present and future signs:

A. Happened and Happening

1. Because of their disobedience, the people of Israel were scattered amongst the nations and had no peace in exile—Deuteronomy 28:64-66.
2. The Jews have returned to their Biblical homeland, however, not all of the Jews have returned, and not to all of what was originally the Promised Land. We can expect to see more Jews returning and there may be further expansion of the current borders of Israel.
3. The formerly desolate land of Israel has become fertile and fruitful—Zechariah 7:14.
4. The Gospel will be preached to all nations—Matthew 24:14. The Gospel is being preached in many nations though not yet in all nations. It may be difficult for us to determine when full coverage has been achieved! At the same time it is surely significant that in a matter of a few years from now the Bible, or parts of it, will have been translated into every language spoken on the earth today.
5. Things will be as they were in the days of Noah and people will be proud, unforgiving, lovers of self, and lovers of money and pleasure (2 Timothy 3:1-5).
6. We can expect that in any communication on end time

prophecies the message, and the messenger, will be mocked and ridiculed (2 Peter 3:3-4).

B. Happening and Yet to Happen

7. Jerusalem will be seen as a problem by the whole world (Zechariah 12:2-3). It is interesting to note that Zechariah made this prophecy in about 520 BC, when Jerusalem was in ruins. Today, as foretold, Israel and Jerusalem are the focus of a massive media coverage that is totally disproportionate to the size of the city or nation.
8. Christians will be persecuted and martyred (Matthew 24:9).
9. Many will turn away from the Christian faith (Matthew 24:10).

C. Yet to Happen:

10. The governance of Jerusalem will be free of Gentile involvement (Luke 21:24).
11. The "Man of Lawlessness" (the Antichrist) will appear on the world stage. He will be seen as a great and very effective unifying world leader (Revelation 13:3-8). He will establish a seven year covenant of peace with Israel which, after 31/2 years, he will break when he declares himself as god in the Temple in Jerusalem.
12. A worldwide financial system will be established requiring people to register and show allegiance to the Antichrist as a prerequisite to being able to shop and trade (Revelation 13:16-17). We hear talk today of a "new world order", globalisation, the need for a worldwide economic management system and a one world government.
13. A 31/2 year period of desolation and despair, the "Great Tribulation", will follow the "Abomination of Desolation" by the Antichrist in the Temple.

14. In order for the prophecy at 13 above to be fulfilled, assuming it is not allegorical, we can expect to see the Temple rebuilt in Jerusalem.
15. All nations will gather to fight against Jerusalem (Zechariah 14:2).
16. Jesus will return and defeat the attacking nations at Armageddon (Zechariah 14:3-4, Revelation 16:14-16, Revelation 19:11, 19-21).
17. The full and awesome realisation that Jesus was and is the Messiah, and all that that implies, will come to the nation of Israel in startling and unmistakeable certainty (Zechariah 12:9-10).
18. The nations will be judged according to their treatment of the Jews (Joel 3:1-2).

I am aware that there can be considerable overlap between these three stages. Furthermore, we may feel something has happened (been fulfilled) only to find that its first "fulfilment" was a model for something much bigger.

I am also aware that this list is my selection and that there are more that could be added. However, time and space dictate a degree of selectivity.

Is it Soon?

This sample list of signs helps to highlight an ambiguity, particularly in respect of those signs that are manifestly not yet fulfilled. The ambiguity, or apparent contradiction, is whether Christ's return can be imminent when there are prophecies yet to be fulfilled. This can cause tension for believers who are serious about observing the signs of the End Times. On the one hand we want to obey the call of Jesus, that we be vigilant and expect his return "at any time". On the other, we want to honour his command to look for the signs that indicate that the time of his return is near. In other words, do the facts indicate that the Parousia is not imminent, or should we be arguing that it is?

I want to briefly list some ways in which Christians try to resolve this tension:

a. Some argue that Jesus won't come at "any time" but at a particular time that can be determined by observing the signs of the End Times (this undermines those teachings that emphasise the surprise of His return).

b. The signs have already been fulfilled (the historicist view).

c. The signs are simply intended to increase our anticipation (Luke 21:28) and devotion, in the hope that we will not be deceived by false prophets and false teachers.

d. The context and emphasis of Jesus' statements suggests that He never intended the signs to be seen as an excuse for not needing to be ready.

e. Jesus will return in two stages; first in secret to "rapture" believers (at "any time" and before fulfilment of all the signs) and then, after the 7 year tribulation, there will be an awesome public return.

f. Similar to e above, but the "rapture" will take place half way through the time of tribulation i.e. at the end of 3½ years of peace, just before the "Abomination of Desolation" and the start of the 3½ years of the great tribulation.

g. Some signs have been fulfilled and those that are still future will happen very quickly.

These suggestions are just that: we will know in in due course which is correct! In the meantime the certainty is that Jesus gave us pointers for the circumstances that will prevail when he returns, but makes it clear that the specific time of his coming cannot be known.

So, we should be alert and watch for these things. Furthermore, we should not be complacent: I may be convinced that there are prophecies to be fulfilled before Jesus returns but that does not mean that I should not be prepared for the possibility of meeting my Lord and Saviour at any moment, whether by rapture or by my demise!

I am convinced that we are well along the time line of prophetic events and that those signs that await fulfilment could happen very quickly. Reading the Bible, constantly watching what is happening, particularly in Israel and Jerusalem, and seeking to understand the spiritual significance of unusual signs and symbolism in the world around us, are all key elements in our being ready for the return of Jesus.

In the next chapter I want to mention one key sign that indicates that we are indeed well along the timeline of the End Times.

I am referring to the rise and spread of radical and very militant versions of Islamic ideology.

Chapter 21: RADICAL AND APOCALYPTIC ISLAM

I have often been asked about the implications of ISIS (Islamic State of Iraq and al Sham (Syria)), also known as IS (Islamic State), or ISIL (Islamic State of Iraq and the Levant), and where it might fit in terms of Biblical prophecy. While it is quite possible that ISIS has little or no significance in relation to Biblical prophecy, I am also convinced that the world faces an unprecedented and largely misunderstood and unacknowledged threat from both "Radical Islam" and "Apocalyptic Islam". I provide in Appendix 2 some background notes on the roots of these two main streams of Islam (known as Sunni and Shi'a).

Let me start by making it absolutely clear that the vast majority of Muslims are peace-loving, law-abiding and blameless. In what follows I am talking about radicalised jihadists and extreme fundamentalists. However, it is an uncomfortable fact that jihadists and fundamentalists are still real Muslims. This cannot and should not be ignored.

The Rise of ISIS

In my concern over events relating to ISIS and Iran, I have felt an increasing pressure to bring people's attention to the dangers of complacency when looking at the rise of ISIS. I don't believe that ISIS members are simply a collection of psychopaths. Some of the "foot-soldiers" may be, but the "generals", the leadership, have clear ideological beliefs, strategies and tactics. Let me quote from an article in the long established, moderate and highly regarded Atlantic magazine:

"Our ignorance of the Islamic State is in some ways understandable: It is a hermit kingdom; few have gone there and returned. Baghdadi has spoken on camera only once. But his address, and the Islamic State's countless other propaganda videos and encyclicals, are online, and the caliphate's supporters have toiled mightily to make their project knowable. We can gather that their state rejects peace as a matter of principle; that it hungers for genocide; that its religious views make it constitutionally incapable of certain types of change, even if that change might ensure its survival; and that it considers itself a harbinger of—and headline player in—the imminent end of the world".

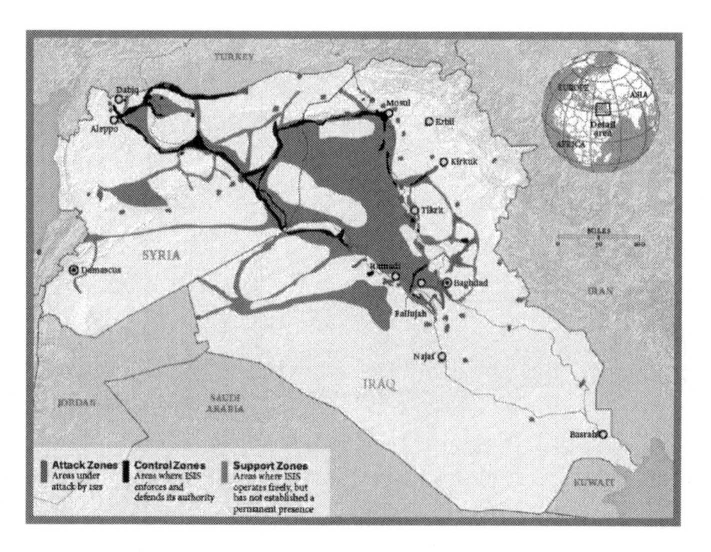

Here is another quote:

"Control of territory is an essential precondition for the Islamic State's authority in the eyes of its supporters. This map, adapted from the work of the Institute for the Study of War, shows the territory under the caliphate's control as of January 15, along with areas it has attacked. Where it holds power, the state collects taxes, regulates prices, operates courts, and administers services ranging from health care and education to telecommunications"

("What ISIS Really Wants," by Graeme Wood, March 2015)

As Graeme Wood suggests, ISIS follows a fundamentalist Islamic creed that leads to a final confrontation that precipitates the return of the Mahdi (the 12th Imam, see Appendix 2 below) the Islamic "messiah".

ISIS seeks to correct what it sees as a mistake of history which allowed western expansion at the expense of Muslim decline.

The correction is seen as dependent on the establishment (re-establishment) of a Caliphate, an expansionist Islamic empire that follows the warfighting strategies and tactics laid down by Mohammad in the 7th century. All ISIS decisions are based on "the Prophetic methodology".

In this respect ISIS has a medieval religious fervour and expansionist commitment following the 7th century precepts of the Prophet in detail.

The West has difficulty understanding this religious fervour which permeates the whole legal and political direction of ISIS. For example, without a caliphate, various aspects of Sharia law do not need to be applied. Once a caliphate exists, however, all the laws apply there and, in theory, all Muslims are obliged to move there. The requirement that the caliph apply all Sharia law includes not recognising borders or negotiating with anyone who has not given allegiance to the Islamic State. In other words, recognition of borders, other nations, international treaties, and so on, would be (already is?) an ideological impossibility for ISIS.

A Caliphate, by definition, requires land and people to lead, and so differs dramatically from the norm of underground terrorist organisations which usually operate in cells or similar covert structures. Furthermore, it is duty-bound both to expand and not to negotiate with infidels.

There lies the challenge!

None of the above answers the question, does ISIS have prophetic significance? However, as watchers or "watch-keepers" I think it is vitally important to seek to understand what is going on and to be alert to the possibility of signs emerging. The Bible covers events in the Middle East, amongst other things, and was written by Middle Eastern authors. The area occupied by ISIS, already greater in size than the UK, is mostly the territory once called Assyria; and their headquarters are in Mosul, which was formerly Nineveh. This means that the site of the former city of Babylon is within ISIS occupied territory.

One thing which I think unlikely is that the Antichrist will arise out of ISIS or a caliphate, as some have suggested. The Antichrist declares himself to be god, which I doubt any true Muslim would do. Initially the Antichrist brings peace and rapprochement to the world, including a treaty with Israel, and I don't see that as compatible with ISIS ideology either.

ISIS and Iran

Most commentators agree that the Shi'a leaders of Iran are seeking to acquire nuclear weapons and certainly they make no secret of their ambition to destroy Israel. Both Iran and ISIS believe that the return of the Mahdi is imminent and both seek to hasten that event, albeit by different routes. ISIS is committing genocide now. Iran seems to be taking a more devious course to nuclear armament with the likely intention of committing genocide later. The Iranian leadership has made little secret of their intent to destroy Israel and also to pursue their goal of a world without the United States, a country they refer to as the "Great Satan."

From Israel's perspective, they are convinced that they face two nation states whose rulers are driven by an apocalyptic, genocidal, End Times eschatology that seeks to annihilate them.

The question for diplomats and negotiators operating on behalf of democratic western nations is whether they can rely on there being any honest intent or integrity in any pledges made by those who actually see it as in their best interests to mislead and prevaricate?

The Return of the Mahdi

The Mahdi or 12th Imam is the anticipated saviour of Islam destined to lead Muslims to world domination. Some Muslim leaders see it as their duty to precipitate the return of the Mahdi by creating a Mahdi army and instigating world turmoil. This Muslim teaching, that Jesus was a prophet who will return, can cause confusion because of its apparent similarity with Christianity.. However, the "Jesus" of Islam is not accepted as Son of God and is foreseen as returning as an assistant of the Mahdi, enforcing conversion to Islam.

The belief in the imminent return of the Mahdi is more prevalent amongst Middle Eastern Muslims than might be expected. According to a poll taken by the Pew Research Centre in 2012, a surprisingly large number of Muslims in Middle Eastern countries believe they will live to see the return of the Mahdi. The figures for this belief by Muslims of the Mahdi's imminent return are: Egyptians 40%; Jordanians 41%; Palestinians 46%; Iraqis 72%.

Figures for those Muslims who believe Jesus will return as a deputy to the Mahdi are: Egyptians 39%; Jordanians 29%; Palestinians 46% and Iraqis 64%.

Christians need to be aware of this parallel and counterfeit version of the return of Christ. We also need to be aware of the political implications of this teaching about a false messiah and a false prophet. The leaders of radical and apocalyptic Islam are seeking to mobilise those who share their End Times views and to convert or destroy those who don't.

ISIS and the End Times

Returning to the question of whether ISIS is an end times "sign", the brutality and warfare of ISIS certainly fulfils Jesus' general predictions of violence in the End Times. Radical and apocalyptic Islam might also be seen as contributors to the urgent need for a peace treaty which will, in fact, be the catalyst for the start of the time of tribulation.

Only time will tell.

Chapter 22: BEING PREPARED

As I write this final chapter, the world is suffering tumultuous disturbances on various fronts. The frequency and severity of natural disasters is increasing exponentially. There are dramatic storms and earthquakes, tsunamis and volcanic eruptions, droughts, famine and plague.

At the same time, political, religious, economic, ethnic and cultural upheavals are also increasing in frequency and severity. The West is emerging from probably the worst and certainly the longest economic crisis it has experienced in modern times: it remains in a fragile debt-riven state of fiscal uncertainty. For the most part, the Third World continues in extreme poverty and deprivation.

The civil war in Syria has lasted for over three years, with no end in view. The war in Afghanistan has resulted in an uneasy and unstable peace. As we discussed in the previous chapter, the troubles in Iraq have taken a turn for the worse as the fundamental Islamist group ISIS is demonstrating extreme barbarism as it expands its control over huge swathes of land in Syria and Iraq.

Israel is surrounded by its enemies and the struggle to contain Hamas-led rocket and tunnel incursions from Gaza continues, although there is a lull as I write. Hamas is labelled as a terrorist organisation by Egypt and the West and recognised as having an avowed intent to destroy Israel.

Egypt is also unstable as it struggles to establish a new government, after disaffection that led to severe internal disruption, rioting and the downfall of the previous "Brotherhood" administration.

As discussed in the previous chapter, there are indications that Iran, a country that is also implacably opposed to the existence of Israel, is developing a nuclear weapons capability.

Russia, a very large but relatively poor and economically challenged country, has a strong dictatorial leader in President Putin. He is flexing his expansionist territorial ambitions in the Ukraine, which may be intended to distract the Russian people's attention from the nation's domestic problems.

America, a relatively rich and strong country, appears to have weak leadership and seems unwilling to take a convincing and forceful role in foreign policy matters.

The loose federal arrangements and vested economic interests in the European Union do not encourage the likelihood of credible united action in circumstances where military intervention might seem appropriate. That leaves the fledgling giant China, which still seems to be concentrating on domestic reorganisation and economic development, but which I expect to see increasing its power and influence on world affairs in the near future.

We see brutal and depraved behaviour, in various trouble spots around the world, and the challenge is whether the perpetrators can be, and in some quarters whether they should be, "policed" by more powerful nations. There are huge ethical and moral questions on what is a justifiable and appropriate response to merciless barbarity. In the absence of strong leadership, and while the issues are debated, we see ever-increasing slaughter and, in relation to displaced people, a humanitarian disaster of unprecedented proportions in the making.

Even as I have been writing, the implications of the Ebola virus, which is devastating regions in West Africa, are becoming more apparent as health experts struggle to find ways to contain the disease.

It could be argued that a fundamental aspect of world unrest is the imbalance in the distribution of wealth. Many people from the poorer nations feel that they have nothing to lose, and desperately want to change the status quo. The wealthy nations, on the other hand, want to protect their trading and general economic advantages.

The interwoven world economic order and the immense cost of modern military warfare undermine the will to engage in military operations and that is, in many ways, a good thing. However, appeasement and a lack of will to defend fundamental democratic principles can encourage ferocious opportunists in the belief that they can operate with impunity. What opposition there is seems to be little more than rhetoric, rather than coordinated and effective action: rhetoric is not an effective deterrent!

I could go on, but I am sure you have the picture. The pace of change is such that this chapter will be out-of-date before it is published!

Ever Ready

At the start of the book I drew attention to the amazing and comprehensive nature of Biblical predictions. There are no other writings, religious or otherwise, that come anywhere close to matching the volume and accuracy of Biblical predictive prophecy.

One of the main objectives of this book is to bring awareness and recognition that the Bible is full of prophecy, from start to finish, and that it is there for a purpose. Biblical prophecy is evidence of God's plan and its fulfilment further validates the truth of His power and authority.

For those looking to confirm that God exists, look no further! To my mind, this level of accurately fulfilled predictions can only be explained by recognising that the Bible is the Word of God, who knows the end from the beginning!

We know what to expect so we can be watchmen and heralds.

My conviction is that the prophetic aspect of God's provision, a fundamental strand of our Christian heritage, has been undervalued and underemphasised for far too long. The evidence is there for all to see. I hope you will join the growing number of people who are willing to broadcast these amazing facts to a world in urgent need of enlightenment.

It truly is time to observe the signs of the End Times.

It is time to be vigilant; it is time to be prepared.

APPENDIX 1: GLOSSARY OF END TIMES TERMINOLOGY

I have tried to avoid using too much theological language in my examination of various signs and prophecies. However, I am aware that if you decide to explore the subject further, you are likely to come across words and expressions that are not in everyday use. I therefore decided it might be helpful to provide a glossary of End Times terminology. The selection is not exhaustive; it is intended in part as a "dictionary" and in part as a brief overview of some of the topics. In some cases the explanations given are matters of fact, while others state commonly held views. A few of the comments involve interpretations and/or opinions that are subject to much conjecture.

Some of the terms and background have been included for completeness, even though the topic has been covered in this book. My hope is that this summary will ease the journey through any subsequent study you may choose to undertake.

Abomination of Desolation – The Antichrist will desecrate the Temple in Jerusalem, claim to be God and set up an image or statue of himself (which will appear to breathe and speak—Revelation 13:14-15). He will demand that he be worshiped (Revelation 13). This is the abomination that leads to great desolation (Mark. 13:14; 2 Thessalonians. 2:3-4). John refers to this image ten times (Revelation 13:14, 15 [three times]; 14:9, 11; 15:2; 16:2; 19:20; 20:4). The abomination is mentioned nine times in Scripture (Daniel 8:13; 9:26, 27; 11:31; 12:11; Matthew. 24:15; Mark 13:14; 2 Thessalonians. 2:3-4; Revelation 13:12-18).

Advent – An arrival or presence, the term "advent" is used in Scripture with reference either to the First or the Second Coming of Jesus, depending on the context.

Antichrist – Antichrist means opposing or false (in place of) Christ. The Antichrist will lead a New World Order (of which the ancient Roman Empire is a shadow). He will be given ability to persecute Israel and the Church for 42 months. (Revelation 13:5). He will oppress Jerusalem for 42 months (Revelation 11:2). The "two witnesses" prophesy in Jerusalem for 1,260 days (Revelation11:3). The remnant of Israel (the "woman" in Revelation 12) will be hidden from the Antichrist in the wilderness for 1,260 days (Revelation 12:6) which is also described as time, times and half a time (Revelation 12:14) and three-and-a-half years (Daniel 7:25). Israel's strength will be devastated (Daniel 12:7). The term "time" refers to 1 year; "times" refers to 2 years and "half a time" to half a year (2 Thessalonians. 2:3-12; 1 John. 2:18, 22; Revelation 13:1-18).

Another Beast – A name for the False Prophet in Revelation 13:11.

Apocalypse – This means unveiling or revealing and is translated as "revelation". It is another name for the Book of Revelation because it unveils or reveals the glory of Jesus and God's End Times plan. In more recent times the word has come to be used as a descriptive noun that indicates damage or destruction on a catastrophic scale.

Apostasy – A falling away or departure from Christian faith (Matthew. 24:9-13; 2 Thessalonians 2:3; 1 Timothy 4:1-2; 2 Timothy 3:1-7; 4:3-4; 2 Peter 2:1-3). An apostate is one who has "fallen away" from the Christian faith.

Babylon – The historical capital of the Babylonian Empire, which was in the lower valley of the Tigris and Euphrates Rivers (now in Iraq). The literalist view of the End Times is that the city of Babylon (fifty miles south of Baghdad) will be rebuilt and used as the headquarters of the Antichrist. It will function as the centre for his worldwide government (Revelation 17-18). Others consider that the term "Babylon" refers symbolically, to the corrupt world political and economic system.

Beast – A term used 36 times to refer to the Antichrist (Revelation13; 14:9-11; 17:3-17; 19:19-21; 20:4, 10).

Daniel's 30 Days – In Daniel 12:11 an angel told Daniel about a thirty-day period that would extend beyond the commonly understood 1,260 days (three and a half years) in which God supernaturally protects the remnant of Israel (Revelation 12:6, 14), the two witnesses prophesy (Revelation 11:3) and the Antichrist persecutes the saints (Revelation 13:5). The "Post Tribulation" (see explanation below) view is that this period ends when Jesus comes in the sky at the seventh trumpet to rapture the saints (Revelation 1:7; Matthew21:30). The 1,290 days shows an additional thirty days after the seventh trumpet during which the Antichrist's rule continues on earth. There is much debate about the 1,335 days mentioned in Daniel 12:12.

Daniel's 70th Week – The final seven-year period before Jesus' Second Coming is referred to as Daniel's 70th week. Daniel prophesied about a "seventy week" period (Daniel 9:24-27). Each "week" was a period of seven years. Therefore these 70 "weeks" of seven years amount to 490 years. This prophecy concerns the timeline of God's plan for the salvation of Israel. The first sixty-nine "weeks" (483 years) were up to the time of Christ's triumphal entry into Jerusalem. We are currently in a pause of the "clock". The last seven-year period will be fulfilled in the lead up to Jesus' Second Coming. It will be initiated when Israel signs a peace treaty with the Antichrist, who will come from (or lead?) the revived Roman Empire (Daniel 9:26-27).

Dragon – Symbolic of Satan in the book of Revelation (Revelation 12:3, 4, 7, 9, 13, 16, 17; 13:2, 4; 16:13; 20:2).

Eschatology – A theological term for the study of End Times as described in Scripture.

False Prophet – The Antichrist's "religious" leader, who will work miracles (Revelation 16:13; 19:20; 20:10). He is called "another beast" in Revelation 13:11.

Fullness of the Gentiles – not to be confused with the "time of the Gentiles" (see below), this phrase is used by the Apostle Paul in Romans 11:25 and refers to a preordained number of Gentiles (i.e. non-Jews) who will choose to believe in Jesus in the timeframe between the First and Second Comings of Christ. Paul teaches that God has set a specific number and that when this has been achieved, His Spirit will begin to lift the veil from the minds of the Jewish people and "all Israel will be saved" (Romans 11:26). The word "fullness" is a mathematical term and indicates that God has a literal number of gentile converts in mind.

Gentiles – Those who are not Jewish by descent and who are regarded by the Jewish people as *ha goyim*—a Hebrew term for "the pagans." It is important to remember that God originally made a covenant with Israel (through Abraham, Genesis 12) and that his plan was to bless all nations of the earth (i.e. the Gentiles) through this, His chosen people. If you are not of Jewish descent, you are a Gentile whatever your specific ethnic background. If you are a Gentile Christian, you are a non-Jewish follower of Jesus. Jewish followers of Jesus are commonly referred to as Messianic Jews today.

Great White Throne Judgment – The time, at the end of the millennial reign, when all unbelievers will be judged by God (Revelation 20:11-15).

Harlot Babylon – The Satan-inspired new world order of government centred in the rebuilt city of Babylon (see above), a symbol of the corrupt world economic system.

Image of the Beast – An image or statue of the Antichrist.

Judgment Seat of Christ – The time when Jesus evaluates the life of all true believers, and rewards them accordingly (2 Corinthians 5:10; Romans 14:10-12). This evaluation occurs immediately after the Church has been raptured. This is also referred to as the Bema judgment, which comes from the Greek word bema which means "judgment seat" or "throne".

Little Horn – A term used by Daniel for the Antichrist (Daniel 7:7-8; 19, 25).

Mark of the Beast – The Antichrist will require everyone to have a mark on his right hand or on his forehead (as a sign of allegiance) in order to buy or sell during the last 3 ½ years of the Tribulation.

Millennium – A 1000-year period when Jesus rules the world. Some believe it is allegorical and are known as "Amillennialists" (i.e. they don't believe the Millennium is a literal 1000 years). Some believe it started when Jesus first came (we are in it, or it is over) and are known as "Post-millennialists". Others take the literal view that it will start when Jesus returns and are known as "Pre-millennialists".

New Jerusalem – The heavenly city where all the saints will live forever in God's immediate presence (Hebrews 11:10, 16; 12:22-24)—after the time of the millennial Kingdom (Revelation 21:2). Please note, this city comes down to the restored earth after the Return of Christ. Believers therefore do not go up to heaven (a common misconception). Heaven comes down to believers. As He did at the First Coming of Christ, Almighty God comes down to where we are to be with us, wiping away every tear from our eyes.

Olivet Discourse – Jesus' prophetic teaching about the End Times found in Matthew 24, Mark 13, and Luke 21, so called because he delivered it on the Mount of Olives

Parenthesis – A pause in the chronology of Revelation, sometimes called "Angelic Explanations", where an angel explains to John the answer to questions arising from the chronological sections.

Parousia – A Greek word meaning the "presence or coming" of an important person. This word is used of Jesus' Second Coming (Matthew. 24:3, 27, 37, 39; 1 Thessalonians. 3:13; 4:15; 5:23; 2 Thessalonians. 2:1, 8; James. 5:7-8).

Post-Tribulation Rapture ("post-trib" for short) – this is the view that the Rapture (see below) and the Second Coming occur at the end of the Great Tribulation. The Church will be on earth during the Great Tribulation.

Preterism – this is the belief that all Biblical prophecies have been fulfilled in the past (the first century AD). The event usually associated with the fulfilment of prophecy is the Roman-Jewish War of AD 66-73, especially the destruction of Jerusalem in AD 70.

Pre-Tribulation Rapture ("pre-trib") – this is the view that the Rapture (see below) occurs before the Great Tribulation. This teaching claims that Christians will not go through the Tribulation.

Rapture – The "gathering in" or "catching away" of God's people in the air when Jesus returns (1 Thessalonians 4:13-18). There is much debate about when and even if this will occur. Suffice it to say, it will be a wonderful event when Christians who have died will be resurrected from their graves to meet Jesus in the sky, followed by Christians who are still left alive on the earth.

Replacement Theology – A hotly debated teaching that the Jews have been rejected by God and that is Israel has been replaced by the church. This view is also known as "supersessionism" (as in the idea that the Church has superseded Israel).

Restrainer – The forces that restrain the Antichrist will be taken out of the way to allow him to come to a place of international political prominence. The idea is that the restrainer functions as the last levy protecting human societies from the tsunami of evil that will overrun the earth when the Antichrist comes. There are at least two views about the restrainer. Post-Tribulation view: this restraining force refers to a combination of two forces referred to by Paul as "someone" and "something" that now restrains the Antichrist (2 Thessalonians. 2:6-8). Paul describes the restrainer of the Antichrist as a "what" (neuter in v. 6) and as a "he" (masculine in v. 7). Thus, the restraining force is a "what" and a "He" working together. Paul taught that the power of the state is appointed by

God to restrain evil (Romans 13:1-4). The "what" that restrains the Antichrist is the power of the state and the "He" is God and His sovereign decree. Pre-Tribulation view: the Holy Spirit is the restrainer that is removed when the Church is raptured before the Great Tribulation (see Tribulation below).

Second Coming of Christ – The time when Jesus will come back physically to rule on the earth. Jesus will travel across the sky when every eye will see Him (Revelation 1:7), then through the land of Edom (Jordan) (Isaiah 63:1-6; Hab. 3:3-16) on to Jerusalem to the Mount of Olives (Zechariah 14:4 ; Revelation 19:17-21). For Post Tribulation believers this is the time the Rapture will occur, at the seventh trumpet which is the last trumpet (Isaiah 27:13; Zechariah 9:14; Matthew 24:31; 1 Corinthians. 15:52; 1 Thessalonians 4:16; Revelation 10:7; 11:15).

Seven Heads – From Daniel 2:41-42; 7:7; Revelation 12:3; 13:1; 17:3-6, these refer to seven world empires throughout history that have persecuted Israel. They are interpreted as being Egypt, Assyria, Babylon, Persia, Greece, Rome, and the revived Roman Empire yet to come—which some equate with the European Union).

Time of the Gentiles – not to be confused with the "fullness of the Gentiles" (see above), this phrase was used by Jesus in Luke 21:24. He said that there that "Jerusalem will be trampled by the Gentiles until the times of the Gentiles will be fulfilled." Notice the context—Jerusalem. Jesus is prophesying here about the destruction of Jerusalem in AD 70 by Gentile invaders (the Roman army). From that time onwards, until a set time in the long term future, Jerusalem and the Temple Mount will continue to be "trampled by Gentiles." Therefore, while the fullness of the Gentiles refers to a spiritual reality (Gentiles becoming born again), the time of the Gentiles refers to a political reality (Gentiles trampling all over Jerusalem). It refers to the dominance of Gentile nations over Jerusalem.

Tribulation – Sometimes used to refer to as the 7 years leading up to the return of Jesus (with the last 3 ½ years being the Great

Tribulation). The first 3 ½ years are expected to be a time of (false) peace when Israel lowers its defenses before the Antichrist reveals his true intentions. So "tribulation" or "great tribulation" more accurately describes the second 3 ½ years (Matthew 24:21, 29; Mark 13:24; Revelation 7:14). Post-Tribulation believers say there is a view that the praying Church will release God's judgments on the Antichrist during the Great Tribulation. In other words, the saints will not be under judgment but rather releasing God's judgments, in much the same way as Moses released God's judgments on Pharaoh.

Two Witnesses – this refers to the two true prophets of God who will stand against the Antichrist by prophesying and testifying during the Great Tribulation (Revelation 11:3-6). They will have similar powers to those of Moses and Elijah (some speculate that they are Moses and Elijah)

Zion – Historically, the hill Mount Zion was the place name for the Jebusite encampment or fortress that King David conquered and where he established his royal capital, the City of David. Over time the name became a metonym for the site of King Solomon's Temple (which most believe was built on Mount Moriah) and eventually for all Jerusalem. The name has poetic, prophetic and spiritual overtones and has come to mean the Jewish homeland. It is symbolic of Jewish national aspiration and the basis for the term Zionism.

APPENDIX 2: BACKGROUND NOTES ON ISLAM

The words *Sunni* and *Shi'a* appear regularly in the media but few non-Muslims understand what these terms really mean.

Religion affects all aspects of life in Muslim countries. The division between Sunnis and Shi'as dates back to a disagreement about who should lead the Muslim community, after the Prophet Muhammad died in AD 632. However, the present nomenclature or designation as Sunni ('one who follows the Sunnah (what the Prophet said, did, agreed to or condemned), or Shi'a (a contraction of the phrase 'Shiat Ali', meaning followers or "partisans" of Ali) came much later.

Within the two groups, Sunni (overall majority of Muslims, approximately 85% of a total of about 2 billion) and Shi'a (majorities in Iran, Iraq and Bahrain, with significant communities in Lebanon, Yemen, Syria, Saudi Arabia, Kuwait and other parts of the Gulf), there are various sects and factions. All agree on the fundamentals of Islam and share the Koran, and the conviction that Muhammad was the last prophet. There are, however, both minor and major differences. The minor differences mostly relate to practice and procedure while the major relate to who inherited, and continues to have, rightful political and religious authority.

Sunnis and Shi'as each have strong claims to the right of succession. Sunnis argue that because Muhammad asked Abu Bakr, a close confidant and senior "Companion" to lead prayers as Muhammad was dying, he was indicating that Abu Bakr should be the next leader.

The basis of the Shi'a claim is that Muhammad announced to

the Companions, on the way back from his last Hajj (pilgrimage to Mecca), that Ali was to lead all believers. Shi'as say Muhammad specified that anyone who followed Muhammad should follow Ali. Ali was Muhammad's son-in-law and cousin, so there was also a claim to succession through the family connection.

In simple terms, the Shi'a claim of inheritance was through a succession of "Imams" (divinely appointed descendants of Muhammad who have absolute spiritual authority). Unlike the Sunni Caliphs (heads of state, political leaders), the Shi'a Imams were religious leaders who were separate from the state. The most prominent group within Shi'a Islam is known as the Twelvers. They believe there have been twelve divinely appointed Imams (descended from Muhammad in the line of Ali and Hussein). They are: Ali, Hassan, Hussein, Ali Zayn al-Abidin, Muhammed al-Baqir, Ja'far al-Sadiq, Musa al-Kazim, Ali al-Rida, Muhammad al-Jawad, Ali al-Hadi, Hasan al-'Askari, and Muhammad al-Muntazar al-Mahdi. The Shi'a believe that the Twelfth Imam, Muhammad al-Muntazar al-Mahdi, was hidden in a cave to avoid capture and persecution and that he disappeared. The Twelver's conviction is that he has been hidden by God and will return as the saviour (Mahdi) of Islam. His disappearance marked the end of the leadership of direct descendants of the Prophet.

In the early days, a few months after Muhammad's death, Ali decided to recognise Abu Bakr as leader, in order to avoid a schism in the fledgling Islamic State.

Ali was eventually chosen as the fourth Caliph and was therefore both Caliph and Imam. He moved the capital of the Islamic state from Medina to Kufa in Iraq. However, his Caliphate was opposed by Aisha, a widow of Muhammad and daughter of Abu Bakr.

After various indecisive battles between the factions, Ali was murdered in AD 661 AD and Mu'awiya became Caliph of the Islamic state. He moved the capital to Damascus. On his death his son Yazid became Caliph.

Meanwhile, the people of Kufa asked Hussein, the son of Fatima (the daughter of Muhammad) and Ali, to be their leader. On his way to Kufa, Hussein was ambushed at Karbala by Yazid's forces. Hussein and his followers were killed in the Battle of Karbala and became martyrs to the Shia cause.

Sunni Development

Sunni Islam Caliphs after Ali were temporal leaders who deferred to religious scholars on spiritual matters. There have been various Caliphate dynasties over the centuries including the Ummayad, the Abbasid, the Mughal and the Ottoman Empires.

Shi'a Development

Since the twelfth Imam, the Shi'a communities have been led by religious scholars, usually referred to as Ayatollahs. As has been said, Shi'a Muslims have always maintained that descendants of the Prophet are the rightful leaders of the Islamic world.

There are significant differences between scholars of Shi'a Islam on the role and power of these representatives. A minority believe the role of the representative is absolute. The majority of Shi'a scholars, however, believe their power is relative and confined to religious and spiritual matters.

The Shi'a have never ruled the majority of Muslims. However, they have had local power and authority from time to time, notably in Egypt, North Africa and Iran (the former Persian Empire).

Conclusion

Most Sunni and Shi'a Muslims have not allowed theological differences to cause antagonism between them. However, there has been an increase in polarisation in recent years, which is a cause for concern.

One of the sects that emerged after the death of the Prophet, the Kharjites, took an uncompromising stance in its interpretation of the Koran. Their fundamentalist approach believed that those who did not accept Islam should either be forced to believe or be eliminated. Their views seem to have resurfaced in the militant jihadist groups of recent years: al-Qaeda (Sunni), Hezbollah (Shi'a), Hamas (Sunni), the Taliban (Sunni), Boko Haram (Sunni) and ISIS (aka the Islamic State) (Sunni).

Made in the USA
Columbia, SC
31 October 2017